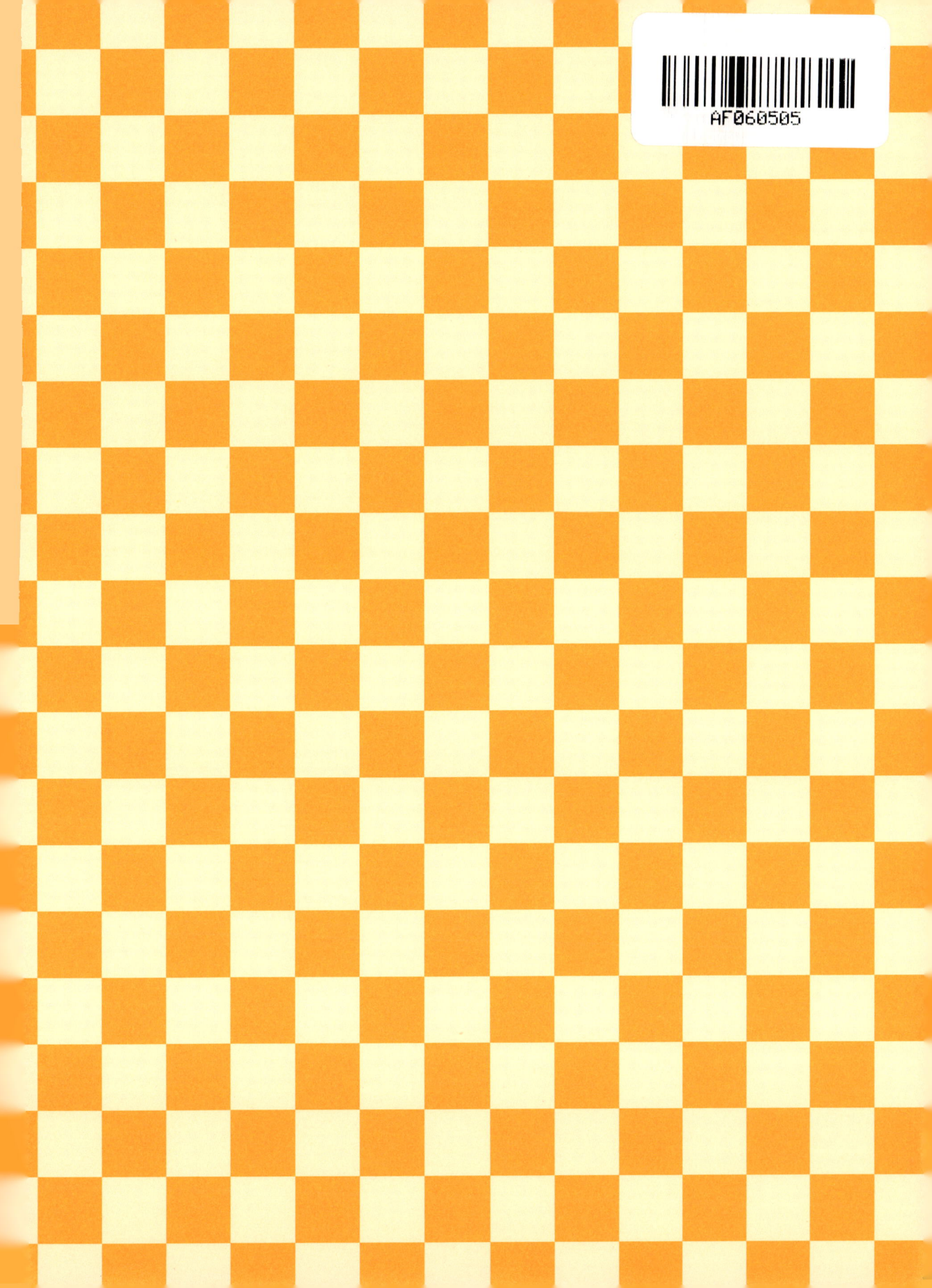

DOPAMINE GARDENING

AMY CHAPMAN

DOPAMINE GARDENING

52 JOYFUL OUTDOOR PROJECTS FOR EVERY SEASON AND ANY SPACE

PAVILION

INTRODUCTION 7

SPRING

29–79

SUMMER

80–133

AUTUMN

134–71

WINTER

172–211

INDEX 212–15
ACKNOWLEDGEMENTS 218
ABOUT THE AUTHOR 219

INTRODUCTION

Gardening isn't something that's always been in my life: I only found it a few years ago when I was lucky enough to move into a little Welsh cottage with a beautiful garden. At the time, I was struggling with anxiety – something that had hindered me throughout my life and often stopped me from doing what I wanted to do. I had tried so many things to ease my symptoms: different types of exercise, yoga, therapy and lifestyle changes. While these methods all helped a little bit, none transformed me in the way that gardening has.

It took me by complete surprise. I started gardening because the lady who had owned the house before me had loved and cared for her garden, and I thought it was only right to look after it too. After a few years of neglect, the garden had been taken over by weeds. So my first task was to start pulling them up, uncovering the beauty beneath that had been so lovingly planted. As I was pulling back the weeds, removing what wasn't serving the garden to allow the plants underneath to thrive, a similar transformation began in me.

It was a near instant metamorphosis. I went from a shy, socially-anxious girl who hid in the corner at gatherings and couldn't answer phone calls or hold conversations with strangers, to someone who came to love throwing herself into scary new situations. To use a cliche garden-related metaphor: gardening had taken an anxious little caterpillar and turned her into a thriving butterfly.

Shortly after dipping my toe into gardening, I started to look into all the possibilities of things I could grow. As someone who had always loved food, it made sense to me that I should try to grow some of my own produce. After all, the best ingredients you can get are those that are freshly picked. The full cycle of growing something from seed to harvest, and cooking delicious, nurturing meals with what you've grown is what really got me hooked on horticulture.

In my first year, I restricted myself to a tiny budget – I didn't know if gardening was going to be just another one of those hobbies where I go in full-steam ahead, buy all of the gear, and then quickly lose interest (see: the crochet yarn, embroidery threads, pottery clay and various niche pieces of exercise equipment in the back of my cupboard). Luckily, you don't actually need to buy much to get started with gardening. A myriad of projects can be done with just a few seeds and some compost. You can reuse old veg packaging to start your seeds in, and even sow seeds you already have in your kitchen cupboard like coriander seeds or chia seeds (see page 182). Thankfully, I've never lost interest in gardening, and I don't know many people who have. It's one of those guilt-free hobbies that makes you feel good, helps the planet and constantly keeps you on your toes. A day in the garden is always a day well spent.

FEEL-GOOD GARDENING

There are so many ways gardening can heal and positively impact your wellbeing, right down to a microbial level. A bacteria in the soil called Mycobacterium vaccae has been shown to stimulate serotonin production – a chemical in our brains which contributes to feelings of happiness and wellbeing. When we put our hands in the soil, the skin absorbs some of this 'happy hormone', which helps to lift our mood.

Studies also show that gardening can trigger the release of dopamine – the 'feel-good hormone' in the reward centre of your brain – which plays a role in memory, mood, motivation and attention. The act of picking fresh produce or even seeing your first strawberry appear in summer releases dopamine, giving us a state of bliss or mild euphoria. This thought dates all the way back to our hunter-gatherer ancestors. But it's not just harvests that make us feel good: the exercise you do while gardening also triggers the release of dopamine. All of this can help us to feel less anxious, improve our memories and make us feel happier – three things I can personally attest to.

Beyond the science, growing plants from seed to harvest and nurturing them along the way gives you a profound sense of accomplishment. This feeling of achievement can then spill out into other areas of life, boosting self-confidence and reminding us that we have the ability to make positive change. It helps to show us that we're capable of more than we may have thought.

Gardening also encourages us to slow down. Many garden tasks, such as weeding, seed sowing and watering are grounding and repetitive, which help us to focus on the present moment. These mindful tasks can also slow down racing thoughts and allow us to work through difficult emotions. It's no wonder people often turn to gardening to cope with grief and difficult circumstances.

And it's not just gardening itself: spending time outdoors, in green spaces, calms us and lifts our mood. Research has shown that the colour green can reduce stress, improve mood and even enhance cognitive function. The simple act of immersing yourself in plants, taking in the birdsong or noticing small changes in the seasons strengthens our connection to the natural world. I find that connecting to nature reminds me I'm a part of something bigger, which can be reassuring when life feels overwhelming. You don't need a huge garden to feel the benefits – even 15 minutes of caring for your houseplants or growing microgreens on your windowsill can make a huge difference to your wellbeing.

On top of all this, there's also the physical side of gardening. The digging, lifting, bending and squatting you do while you're out in the garden doesn't feel like exercise at the time, but it's a diverse form of gentle movement that helps to keep the body active. Combined with the fresh air and natural daylight, this physical activity can improve sleep, increase energy levels and support overall wellbeing.

Perhaps one of the most powerful things about gardening is the hope it brings. Sowing a seed is a tiny act of faith in the future. It helps us to remember that something good is coming. Whether you're waiting for flowers to bloom or for your first tomato to ripen, there's always something to look forward to.

GARDENING IN ANY SPACE

I'm a firm believer that you don't need a lot of space to start gardening. You don't even need a garden! Of course, being able to grow ten different varieties of tomato is lovely, but a lot can be done in compact spaces too. Don't underestimate the difference a few pots on a windowsill or balcony could make to your home and lifestyle. In just a square metre, you could be self-sufficient in salad leaves year-round, allowing you to reduce food miles and add homegrown fresh harvests to every meal (see page 105), or in just a single pot you could grow a variety of herbs to make your own teas and toiletries (see pages 94–5, 82, 86 and 154).

I love getting creative and packing as many plants into small spaces as possible. Layering different types of plants – such as climbers, tall plants and shorter ground cover plants – is a great way of utilizing every level of space you have. You could also opt for compact versions of your favourite plants: there are some tomato varieties that are small enough to grow on a windowsill and even dwarf apple trees that can be grown in pots.

Small-space gardening has its advantages too. It allows you to focus on what's in front of you, notice small changes in the plants and spend extra time perfecting your space. You're more likely to spot a brand-new bud that's about to burst into life, or a slug on your lettuce which can be swiftly (but gently) removed.

Many of the projects in this book are suitable for small gardens, balconies and even indoors:

- Grow chamomile from a teabag (page 28)
- Make wildflower seed paper (page 43)
- Grow your own plant pots (page 68)
- Grow your own salad bar (page 105)
- Flower hammering (page 112)
- Make a bulb lasagne (pages 144–5)
- Grow mushrooms on coffee grounds (page 174).

So whether you've got a tiny courtyard, a few pots by the back door or a sunny windowsill, there's plenty you can do. Gardening isn't about the size of the space, it's about being creative, making the most of what you have and finding joy in the little things.

IN HARMONY WITH NATURE

One of the greatest joys of gardening is seeing the impact you can have on wildlife. Just adding a few flowering plants to your space can bring in bees and butterflies, and piling up leaves or logs over winter can create homes for bugs. When you see that something you've created can help wildlife to thrive, it can give you a real sense of purpose.

Pollinators are more at threat now than ever before, due to heavy use of pesticides and habitat loss. Creating a little haven for wildlife in your garden could be essential for their survival. Even small gardens can provide food, water and shelter for birds, insects and mammals, which can help your local ecosystems to thrive.

The key to gardening in a way that's kind to the earth is to practice reciprocity. Make sure to never take more than you put in. Each time you harvest something, practice gratitude and thank Mother Earth for what she's provided you. This mindset helps us to foster a kinder, gentler relationship with the earth.

The little moments of joy we get to observe when we invite wildlife in — from the first butterfly in spring to bees sleeping in flowers and tadpoles growing into frogs — can help us to connect with nature on a deeper level. This connection has been shown to provide psychological benefits, such as reduced stress, greater creativity and improved wellbeing. By looking after the earth, she is looking after us.

SOME TIPS FOR CREATING WILDLIFE-FRIENDLY GARDENS:

- Lay off pesticides and herbicides, even organic ones
- Plant a diverse garden with a variety of flowers and plants
- Sow native plants, trees and wildflowers
- Don't keep your garden too tidy, allow grass to grow long to create habitats
- Provide water sources – even a small dish of water can make a huge difference

I'VE FEATURED LOTS OF WILDLIFE-FRIENDLY PROJECTS THROUGHOUT THE BOOK, SUCH AS:

- Pollinator Planting (page 32)
- Create a Container Pond (page 97)
- Make an Olla Insect Bath (page 108)
- Plant a Night Scented Garden (page 131)
- Build a Bee Mansion (page 177)
- Make a Wildlife Teepee (page 187)
- Craft DIY Bird Feeders (page 190)

These projects all help to invite wildlife in, giving them the food, water and habitat they need to survive.

HAVE FUN WITH IT

One of the biggest lessons gardening has taught me is that I need to let go of things I can't control. There are so many variables in the garden (sunshine, rain, wind, pests, diseases, temperature and soil, to name a few) which mean we can't always predict what's going to happen. To be a successful gardener, you must accept that not everything will go to plan. Sometimes plants will die, and the best thing you can do is observe, learn from it and try again.

The multitude of variables can sometimes play in our favour. We all have slightly different soils and microclimates, and the weather can change drastically from year to year, which means there's no one rulebook that will work for everyone. By all means, use the information on seed packets, websites and this book as a guide, but don't stress too much about exact timings. My biggest piece of advice to anyone looking to start their gardening journey is... don't take it too seriously! I like to treat every project as a little experiment, often bending the typical garden rules to see what I can achieve.

Time spent in the garden is never wasted. Yes, it may be a little sad if the tomato plant you've been nurturing for months dies because you forgot to water it, but the time you spent caring for it wasn't wasted. While you were caring for your plant, the garden was giving back to you. You were getting fresh air, your hands in the soil and gentle exercise.

The inevitable mishaps you encounter while gardening help to foster resilience. When things go wrong, you learn how to pick yourself up and carry on. Each mistake you make teaches you a valuable lesson — it could be to protect certain plants from slugs, or that one of your plants needs a lot more water than you thought. Each lesson will help to make you a better gardener. This learning curve can also extend outside of gardening. In life, things won't always go to plan; the important thing is that you pick yourself up, learn to adapt and carry on. It's freeing to realize that even if you don't win every battle, the garden (and you) can still thrive.

At the end of the day, gardening should be fun. Your garden doesn't need to be perfect, and you certainly don't need to be an expert before you begin. Some of the most joyful moments in the garden come from experimenting, playing with ideas and seeing what happens. You never know what the garden will surprise you with. This book has been created with beginners in mind, so even if you're brand new to gardening, you'll find plenty of ideas here to get you started. Gardening isn't about getting everything right, it's about enjoying the process and seeing where it takes you.

The following projects are designed to make you feel good and help you find joy. Whether from creating something fun and satisfying like plant pots grown from mycelium (see page 68), or helping you to feel calm by working with relaxing aromatic herbs like lavender (see page 92). The book is packed with 52 fun, creative and calming projects, split across all four seasons. In spring, you could plant a healing windowsill garden (page 51) to create your own simple remedies for common ailments; in summer you could sow a herbal tea garden (pages 94–5) to blend your own relaxing or mood-boosting teas; in autumn, compile a mushroom tower (page 165) for an easy and satisfying way to grow your own mushrooms; and in winter, you could construct a wildlife teepee (page 187) to provide a habitat to help wildlife survive the colder months. To feel the mood-boosting benefits of gardening year-round, you could do one project each week of the year. So, whether you're a complete beginner who's never gardened before, or you're looking for fun, creative horticultural ideas to try, you'll find plenty of inspiration in this book. My hope is that you find joy and happiness from these projects, and that maybe you too will feel the mood-boosting benefits of gardening.

GARDENING GLOSSARY

Below are the valuable skills and knowledge that will help set you up for success with the projects in this book and throughout your gardening journey.

COMPOST
The most important ingredient in any gardening recipe, compost is a growing medium made from decaying organic matter. Getting compost right can be the difference between whether your plants thrive or barely survive.

PEAT-FREE COMPOST
Always look for peat-free compost, as peat extraction destroys animal habitats and releases carbon.

MULTIPURPOSE COMPOST
The most versatile type of compost, widely available and great for container plants, mulching and general use.

SEED COMPOST
A finer texture than multipurpose compost and lower in nutrients. Specially formulated to give seeds the best start but shouldn't be used to grow in long term.

HOMEMADE COMPOST
Made for free using kitchen scraps, garden waste and any other organic materials you can get your hands on. Very nutrient-dense so works well as a soil improver, mulch or mixed with other soil/multipurpose compost in pots for very hungry plants.

FREE DRAINING
A term used for soil or compost that doesn't hold onto excess water, allowing water to pass through. This prevents roots from sitting in soggy conditions and rotting. Mixing soil with grit, perlite, sand or organic matter improves drainage.

FROST DATES/FIRST AND LAST FROST
Frost can kill tender plants, so check your area's average last frost date online, and keep an eye on the weather forecast. You can plant out tender plants once all risk of frost has passed. Finding out the average first frost date and keeping an eye on the forecast towards the end of the growing season can help inform you on whether you need to bring tender plants indoors or protect them with horticultural fleece.

MULCH
A layer of material (like compost, bark or woodchip) spread over the soil surface. This locks in moisture, suppresses weeds, improves soil health and adds nutrients to the soil as it breaks down. It can also protect roots from extreme temperatures.

SEED SOWING
Check the information on the seed packet for guidance as different seeds have different needs. A good rule is to sow seeds at a depth of twice the size of the seed. Try to keep compost moist – you can use a clear plastic bag or propagator lid to lock in moisture – and be patient as some seeds can take a long time to germinate.

DIRECT SOWING
This is when you plant seeds straight in the ground where they'll grow.

SOWING UNDER COVER
Using a greenhouse, cold frame or polytunnel for extra protection.

SOWING INDOORS
Starting seeds inside your house on a sunny windowsill or with grow lights to give them as much light as possible. Great for tender plants that need a head start e.g. chillies and aubergines.

HARDENING OFF
If you've started your seeds under cover or indoors, they may need to be gradually acclimatized to outdoor conditions before they're planted out. This means putting the seedlings outdoors for a few hours during the day, and then bringing them back in for the night over a week or so.

WATERING
It's generally a good idea to water plants deeply and less often, rather than little and often, as this helps them to develop strong, deep roots. Watering in the early morning or evening is best, as it means less water will be lost to evaporation.

THINNING OUT
Sometimes it's worth sowing a couple of seeds into each pot for best chances of germination. If both germinate, remove the smaller, weaker seedling to give the remaining one the best chance of survival. When sowing some seeds directly (e.g. carrots) it's also worth sowing them quite thickly to account for poor germination or pest damage; these may also need to be thinned out to give the remaining seedlings enough space to grow.

MAKING COMPOST
I try not to overcomplicate the compost-making process; people often get overwhelmed by the ratios of ingredients or how often to turn it, but it's easy to forget that compost is something that happens in nature, and nature doesn't always get the exact ratios right. To make compost, layer 'greens' (soft, fresh materials e.g. veg scraps, grass clippings) with 'browns' (dry, woody materials e.g. cardboard, dry leaves) in a compost bin or heap and let nature do the work of breaking it down. I do roughly half and half of greens and browns. Turning the pile every so often helps to speed up the process by adding air to the mix.

ANNUAL VS PERENNIAL PLANTS
Annuals complete their whole life cycle in a year (they germinate, flower, set seed and die) so need to be started again each season. Perennials live for many years, they often take a little longer to establish but will reward you year after year.

COMPANION PLANTING
Some plants grown together can help each other by deterring pests or attracting beneficial insects. For example, planting marigolds with tomatoes has been shown to deter whiteflies.

TRAP CROPS
Trap crops are sacrificial or decoy plants that are grown to divert pests away from your main crop, so that your prized plants are left alone. I commonly use nasturtiums, which help to keep aphids and caterpillars away from my brassicas.

SPRING

Spring has to be my favourite season of the year – there's so much hope and anticipation in the air. It really is the season of new beginnings. As soon as I see the first snowdrop shoots poking up through the soil, I start getting excited about everything that's to come. After what often feels like a very long winter, this is when the garden finally wakes up. I find so much joy in early spring's small details – the buds on the trees, the first seedlings germinating and bugs appearing from their little hiding places. Things really start to pick up speed as the season continues – the daylight hours rapidly get longer and everything suddenly bursts into life. Spring is the time to get things going again, to start planting and sowing seeds for the year ahead, and to set the garden up for success.

GROW CHAMOMILE FROM A TEABAG

Chamomile has been used medicinally for thousands of years to calm anxiety and settle stomachs. It's also used as a mild sedative to help with issues such as difficulty falling or staying asleep. And luckily, you might already have everything you need to grow your own chamomile plants. If you've got a packet of chamomile teabags at the back of your kitchen cupboard, you can use these to grow an endless supply of herbal tea so you'll never have to buy the bags again. This works because chamomile tea is brewed with flower heads, and when these are harvested, some of them will already contain viable seeds. From one teabag, you can expect to grow at least four chamomile plants. This won't work with regular tea or most herbal teas as these are usually brewed with leaves.

WHAT YOU'LL NEED
Seed tray
Seed compost (I mix my own using multipurpose compost, coco coir and vermiculite)
1–2 chamomile teabags
Clear plastic lid to cover your seed tray, or a clear polythene bag/sandwich bag large enough to fit the seed tray
A sunny spot in your garden 30cm², with free-draining soil

WHEN TO START
Plant out in late spring

WHEN TO ENJOY
Early summer to early autumn

1 Fill your seed tray to the top with seed compost, then water so that the compost is evenly moist throughout. Allow excess water to drain away.

2 Tear your teabag(s) open, then sprinkle the contents in an even layer across the surface of the compost. Teabags contain a mix of other parts of the flower head too, like petals, so you can sow them quite thick so they almost cover the whole surface of the soil, much thicker than you would usually sow seeds.

3 Gently press the seeds down so they get good contact with the compost. Chamomile needs light to germinate, so you don't want to completely bury the seeds.

4 Cover the seed tray with a clear lid or polythene bag to keep the moisture in, until the seeds germinate.

5 Place the seed tray on a sunny windowsill — chamomile germinates at about 19°C so it's usually best to start the seeds off indoors.

6 Check every day to make sure the compost isn't drying out. I like to 'bottom water' my chamomile seeds/seedlings, as it stops the seeds from being displaced and ensures the compost is all evenly moist. Just place the seed tray in a shallow tray of water or in a sink filled with 1cm water, and the compost will absorb the water from the bottom up.

7 Keep on top of watering as the seedlings germinate, and once you can see roots at the bottom of the seed tray and all risk of frost has passed, you can plant them out into your sunny spot in the garden.

8 Chamomile blooms from early summer, so you can harvest the flowers as soon as they're fully open to make your own delicious homegrown herbal tea.

POLLINATOR PLANTING

I'm sure we all know by now the important role that pollinators play in our ecosystems – they facilitate plant reproduction which is essential to our food systems. Pollinators are also vital for the reproduction of wild plants which, in turn, help more of our wildlife survive. So, what could be a better use of your time and garden space than creating a pollinator patch? You'll be helping bees and other important insects by providing them with nectar, which will give them the energy they need to survive. You'll also have a direct impact on your local ecosystems. In a time where much of the countryside has been taken over by monocultures sprayed with pesticides, your little patch will become a haven for these much-needed insects.

WHAT YOU'LL NEED
An area of your garden, or a container to plant into
A variety of different flowering plants that bloom throughout the year (see opposite)
Peat-free multipurpose compost

WHEN TO START
Plant out in late spring

WHEN TO ENJOY
Year-round

1 Choose where to put your pollinator patch. You can make this as big or small as you like – a large garden bed would provide ample food for many bees, butterflies and other insects, but a small planter or window box could be life-saving for pollinators searching for food in a city. You can locate it in either full sun or part shade, just make sure to check plant labels and choose plants that are suited to the conditions that you'll be growing in.

2 Choose your flowers. Different pollinators like to consume nectar from different shaped flowers, so try and mix it up with tubular-shaped specimens such as foxgloves, those with open blooms such as cosmos, or plants with lots of tiny flowers grouped together, like buddleja. It's also a good idea to try and get plants that bloom at different times of the year, so you can provide pollinators with food year-round.

3 Prep the growing space. If you're growing in-ground, pull up any large or aggressive weeds to give your plants the best chance of success. If you're growing in a pot or container, make sure it has holes in the bottom to allow water to drain out so your plants don't rot. Fill your container up most of the way with compost, leaving enough space for your plants.

4 Take your plants out of their pots, being careful not to damage them and transfer them into your growing area, giving each one enough space to grow. Backfill around the plants with compost.

5 Give your plants a good water, and water every few days during dry spells.

6 Sit back and wait for your plants to bloom and for pollinators to enjoy them. See what types of pollinators you can spot, you might see different types of bees, butterflies, hoverflies and more.

SUMMER
monarda (also known as bee balm), chives, alliums, fennel, Ammi majus, marigolds, sunflowers

AUTUMN
salvia, sedum, perennial wallflower, honeysuckle, heather, dahlias

SPRING
crocus, lungwort, rosemary, fritillaries, anemones, daphne

WINTER
snowdrops, hellebores, winter aconite, witch hazel, iris reticulata, camellias

CREATE A COCKTAIL GARDEN

Life's too short to grow boring plants, so why not grow a cocktail garden? Choose fragrant plants to flavour your favourite cocktails and mocktails. You won't believe how much flavour you can get from a few leaves picked fresh from a homegrown herb plant. You could even throw your own cocktail party! Invite your friends round to try out some of your very own herbs and get creative with the drinks you make.

WHAT YOU'LL NEED
An area of your garden or large planter – full sun is ideal for this
A selection of different flavoured plants, you could use herbs, fruits or even edible flowers
Peat-free multipurpose compost

WHEN TO START
Plant out in late spring

WHEN TO ENJOY
Spring, summer and autumn

1 Choose where to put your cocktail garden. The plants I've listed below thrive in full sun, so it's a good idea to choose a nice sunny spot to plant them in. You could choose a large container for your cocktail garden – something similar to a half whiskey barrel would work well, or you could plant directly into the ground.

2 Prep the growing space. Try and remove the majority of the weeds from the area if you are planting your cocktail garden in-ground. If you're planting into a container, make sure it has drainage holes and fill it part of the way with multipurpose compost, leaving enough space for your plants.

3 Remove your plants from their pots, and plant directly into your container or prepared growing area, just make sure to give each plant plenty of room to grow. Give everything a good water, straight after planting. Keep on top of watering as the plants grow, especially during dry periods.

4 Harvest the plants as and when you need them, and get creative with your cocktail making!

COCKTAIL GARDEN PLANTS

Lemon verbena
Rosemary
Thyme
Mint
Lavender
Sage
Strawberries
Cucumbers
Borage
Calendula

TIP: Plant mint in a separate pot, and never into the ground as it tends to take over.

RECIPE IDEA: LEMON VERBENA MOJITO

Once you've planted up your cocktail garden, there are so many possibilities of drinks you could make. Many of the plants are great for teas and desserts too. One of my favourite things to make from my cocktail garden is this lemon verbena mojito. The mint, lemon verbena and lime make it so refreshing and uplifting. You can either have it boozy, or switch to alcohol-free rum for a mocktail version.

½ lime, cut into wedges
2 tsp light brown sugar
10 lemon verbena leaves, plus extra to garnish
5-10 mint leaves
Crushed ice
50ml white rum (or alcohol-free alternative)
Soda water (to top up)

1 In a sturdy glass, muddle the lime wedges with the sugar to release the juice.

2 Add the lemon verbena and mint leaves and gently bruise them to release their oils.

3 Fill the glass with crushed ice.

4 Pour in the rum and top up the glass with soda water.

5 Stir well and garnish with the extra lemon verbena leaves.

SUNFLOWER GROWING CHALLENGE

There's something so joyful about sunflowers to me, their round faces always turning to smile at the sun; I could never be sad in a field full of sunflowers! So why not involve your friends and family in a little sunflower growing competition? The challenge element of this project helps to get everyone invested in their plants, making sure they nurture them as they grow. The more competitive people get with this one the better — you could come up with creative tactics to help your sunflower grow, like making your own fertilizer or even talking to your plant. Just please, no sunflower sabotage!

WHAT YOU'LL NEED
A weed-free area of the garden in full sun or large plant pots
Peat-free, multipurpose compost or well-rotted manure
Sunflower seeds
Plant labels or lollipop sticks
Permanent marker or pencil

WHEN TO START
Late spring (after last frost)

WHEN TO ENJOY
Enjoy the process of cheering your plant on from spring, all the way until it blooms in late summer

1 Choose where to grow your sunflowers; an area in full-sun is best; this could be in a flower bed or large plant pots. Prepare the area by removing weeds and adding plenty of compost or well-rotted manure.

2 Poke two seeds (in case one doesn't germinate) into the ground about 2cm deep for every participant. Space each participant's seeds about 45cm apart to allow the plants plenty of room to grow.

3 Don't forget to label each plant, so you know who they belong to, and give everything a good water.

4 If both seeds from each planting site germinate, remove the weaker seedling, leaving you with one plant every 45cm.

5 Now, it's up to you how you cheer your plant on and what methods you use to encourage growth. Whether that's regular watering, talking to your plant, or even making your own supercharged compost to feed them with.

6 When your sunflowers bloom, make sure to measure them to see whose grows the tallest! You could give out a prize for the winner and keep a record of the heights to try and beat them next year!

1

4

5

5

7

MAKE YOUR OWN WILDFLOWER SEED PAPER

This seed paper is perfect to use for cards, crafts and gifts. It's fun and easy to make, and a great activity to do with kids. You could decorate this however you like: add in dried flower petals to make it even prettier, cut the paper into different shapes, or add your own drawings to it. I love using British native wildflowers in my seed paper to help with biodiversity and food for pollinators, but you could add any seeds you like – even vegetable seeds like lettuce will work!

WHAT YOU'LL NEED
Scrap paper
Large bowl
Water
Blender
Wildflower seeds
Dried flower petals (optional)
Paper-making screen
Paper towel or old newspaper
Tea towel

WHEN TO START
Any time

WHEN TO ENJOY
Year-round, but plant the seed paper in spring or autumn

1 Rip up your scrap paper into small pieces and add to your bowl. Cover with water (at a ratio of approx. one part paper to ten parts water) and leave to soak overnight.

2 The next day, blend the paper and water mixture until smooth with no large lumps.

3 Stir in your wildflower seeds. If using petals for decoration, add these in too.

4 Put your paper-making screen in the sink and pour over the seed and paper mixture. Spread the mixture evenly across the screen and allow as much moisture to drain away as possible.

5 Lay out a tea towel on a flat surface, then open your paper making screen and flip it over onto the tea towel. Gently press the back of the screen with a piece of paper towel or old newspaper to help remove excess moisture and release the pulp from the screen.

6 Place the tea towel in a warm, well ventilated area until dry.

7 Once dry, remove the paper from the tea towel and use in crafts as you please.

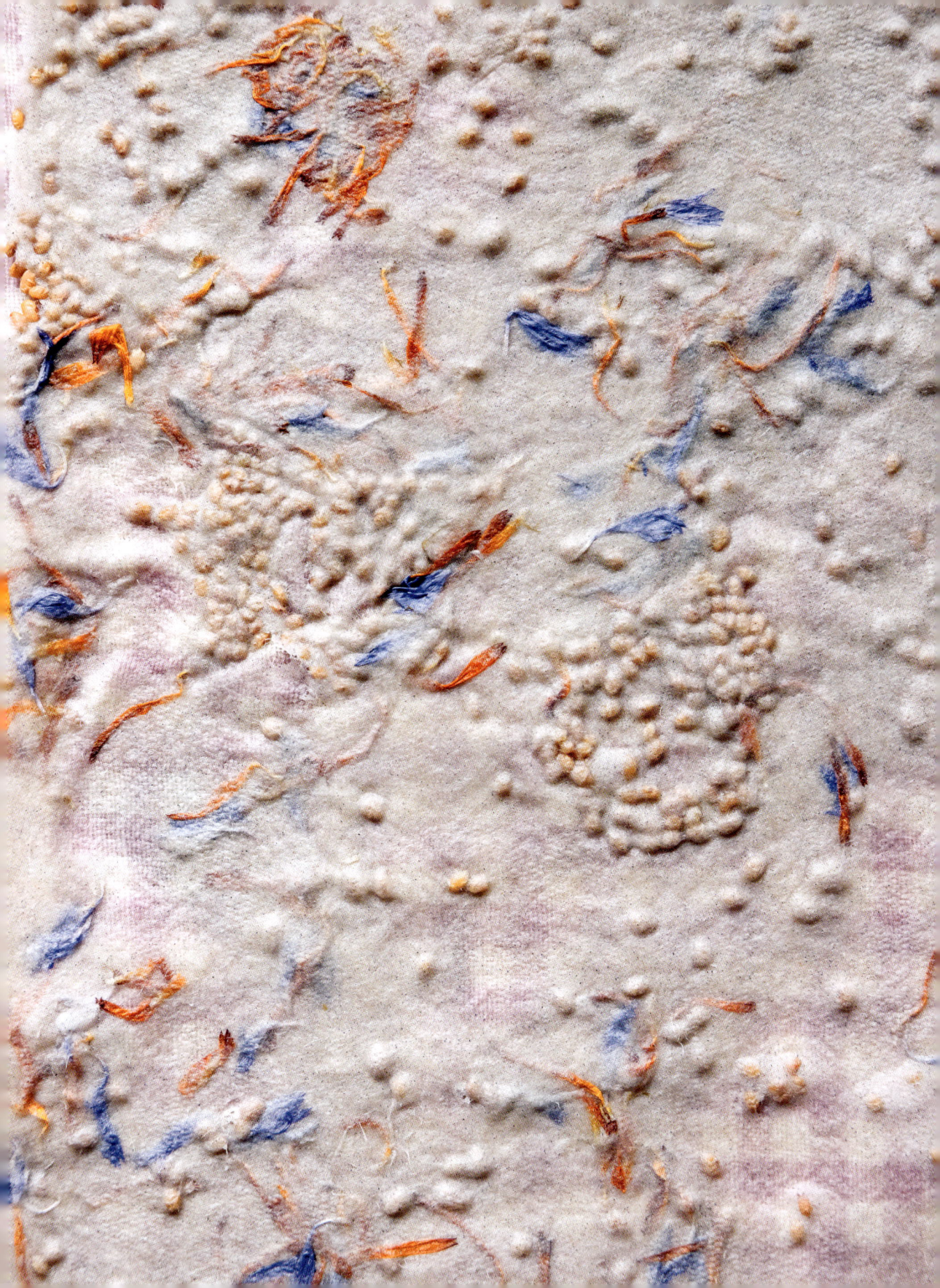

PLANT A NOSTALGIA PATCH

Some plants just have a way of taking you right back. Every time I see gunnera, I'm reminded of my nan's garden and the huge, towering plant that me and my siblings used to hide under when we were playing. When I feel the silky soft leaves of Lamb's Ear, I'm transported to the times I spent playing with my little Playmobil figures in my mum's back garden. These are such specific memories, which are made all the more vivid with the help of plants. This is why I love the idea of planting your own nostalgia garden. It should be a little selection of plants that bring you back to memories from your childhood, perfect to go and look at when you're feeling a little down.

WHAT YOU'LL NEED
Any plants that bring back happy memories
A large plant pot or container
Peat-free multipurpose compost

WHEN TO START
Late spring (depending on plant selection)

WHEN TO ENJOY
Summer (depending on plant selection)

1 Read the labels on your plants to check what their needs are and make sure they're suitable for planting together.

2 Prepare your pot or container by filling it with peat-free multipurpose compost, leaving a few centimetres free at the top.

3 Remove your plants from their pots and plant into the container, making sure you give them enough room to grow.

4 Place your pot in its final position, ideally somewhere you'll walk past often.

5 Water the plants in and make sure you keep on top of watering when the top few centimetres of soil feel dry.

TIP: Try to choose plants that like the same growing conditions as each other if you're planting them in the same pot. For example, only choose plants that like full sun if your pot is going to be in the sunniest section of your garden. Otherwise, you could plant up a couple of smaller pots or containers to suit each plant's needs.

MAKE A 'SECRET GARDEN' ARCHWAY

I find secret and hidden gardens so magical. It's so exciting discovering what beautiful plants are hiding around the corner. I grew up watching *The Secret Garden* film, where three children find an abandoned walled garden and begin to tend to it, transforming not only the garden but their mindsets too — they become happier and healthier as a result of their interactions with nature. This garden archway project is an homage to secret gardens. Creating a beautiful entrance to your garden sets the tone for the time you spend there, and it will entice you to wander through it too.

WHAT YOU'LL NEED
Four or more freshly cut hazel, willow or birch branches, at least 2.5m long
String
Scissors
Compost
Seeds for climbing plants — sweet peas, peas or climbing beans work well

WHEN TO START
Early spring

WHEN TO ENJOY
Throughout summer

1 Make the main arch structure by pushing your branches into the soil. I like to make my archways just over 1m wide, and use at least two branches on each side. Push the branches into the ground as far as they will go, and make sure they're really secure.

2 Bend the branches over at the top, twisting them around the opposite branch if possible, and secure in place with string.

3 Add horizontal rows of branches to the archway for more stability and to give your plants something to cling to as they climb up, secure these in place with string.

4 Add a good dressing of compost at the base of your archway.

5 Poke your climbing plant seeds into the ground about 2cm deep at 20cm intervals along the foot of the archway and water them.

6 As your plants begin to grow, they may need some help to find the archway, so loosely tie them to the structure with string.

7 Keep on top of watering during dry spells and wait for the plants to scramble up and over the archway.

3

5

7

CREATE A HEALING WINDOWSILL GARDEN

It was important to me to make sure I included lots of small-space projects in this book – and this windowsill garden is one of them! If you don't have access to a garden, I'd recommend making use of your windowsills for growing useful plants and those that bring you joy. I've suggested a mix of healing plants for this project to help with anything from sunburn to indigestion.

WHAT YOU'LL NEED
Five or more pots or recycled containers with drainage holes and saucers to stand them on
Peat-free multipurpose compost
Seeds or small plants (see box for suggestions)
Plant labels or lollipop sticks
Permanent marker or pencil

WHEN TO START
Early spring

WHEN TO ENJOY
Year-round

1 Fill each pot with compost, leaving a gap of a few centimetres at the top.

2 Sow seeds into the pot according to the instructions on the seed packet (you usually sow seeds at a depth of two times the size of the seed).

3 Or, transplant shop-bought plants into the pots and firm in.

4 Label each pot so you don't forget which plant is which.

5 Gently water the seeds/plants.

6 Place the pots on a bright, sunny windowsill and remember to water the soil so it doesn't dry out.

7 Harvest as needed.

HEALING PLANTS

Chamomile
Calming, aids digestion, soothes skin

Calendula
Anti-inflammatory, soothes skin, aids digestion

Mint
Cooling, aids digestion

Aloe vera
Treats skin conditions, sunburn relief

Lemon balm
Mood boosting

Thyme
Anti-inflammatory, antimicrobial, antiseptic

GROW YOUR OWN HALLOWEEN PUMPKIN

Pumpkins are one of the most satisfying plants to grow. Nothing quite beats the sense of achievement when you harvest your first big beautiful pumpkin! There are so many fun pumpkin varieties you can choose from too. Whether you want to grow a giant classic orange Halloween pumpkin, a funky blue or a spooky warty variety, you're sure to find something that excites you.

WHAT YOU'LL NEED
9cm plant pot
Good-quality compost
Pumpkin seeds
A weed-free area of your garden, at least 1m², in full sun
Tiles or bricks

WHEN TO START
Mid to late spring

WHEN TO ENJOY
Autumn

1 Fill your 9cm plant pot with compost and poke two seeds in.

2 Water your pot, then place on a sunny windowsill inside to germinate, continuing to water the pot if the top 2cm of soil dries out.

3 If both of the seeds germinate, remove and discard the weaker looking seedling.

4 Once all risk of frost has passed, start to 'harden off' your pumpkin plant (see page 22).

5 Prepare the planting area by removing all weeds, digging a large hole, and adding in at least a bucket full of compost.

6 Remove your pumpkin plant from its pot and plant into the prepared ground, being careful not to disturb the roots.

7 Pumpkins love water, so make sure to give them a good drink every few days during dry spells.

8 When fruits start to form, place a tile or brick underneath to keep them off the damp soil and prevent rotting.

9 Keep the pumpkins on the plant for as long as possible, but make sure to harvest them before the first frost. Cut the pumpkins with at least 10cm of stem still attached in a 'T' shape, to prevent rotting.

10 For longer storage, place your pumpkins in a warm, sunny spot for 7–10 days to cure.

FOR GIANT PUMPKINS:
- Feed plants with an organic fertilizer every couple of weeks, making sure to dilute it according to the manufacturer's instructions.
- Limit the number of fruits to 2-3 per plant. Once the fruits have started forming, remove any extra flowers to divert all energy to the fruits.

GROW A WICKED WITCH'S GARDEN

I've always been fascinated by witches – they held so much ancient knowledge about plants, herbal remedies and even poisons. For this project, you can take it in a healing direction by choosing helpful plants to heal your ailments, or you could go down a slightly darker route and opt for poisonous plants, just remember to wash your hands after handling them!

WHAT YOU'LL NEED
An area of your garden to plant into
Peat-free multipurpose compost
A variety of witchy plants

WHEN TO START
After the last frost

WHEN TO ENJOY
Summer to autumn

1 Prepare your garden bed by removing all weeds.

2 Add a thick layer of peat-free multipurpose compost to enhance soil fertility.

3 Remove your witchy plants from their pots and plant into the bed, leaving some space between them to allow them to grow larger.

4 Give everything a really good water.

5 Enjoy your enchanting witchy garden.

WITCH'S GARDEN PLANTS AND THEIR USES

Yarrow
Wound healing, love potions, protection against evil

Foxglove
Used in heart medication, but also extremely poisonous

Mugwort
Used to enhance dreams

Fennel
Hung over doorways to protect against evil spirits

Poppy
Used to induce sleep and promote fertility

Sage
Used to dispel negative energy and purify spaces

PRODUCE WEIRD AND WONDERFUL VEGETABLES

Growing my own food was my gateway into gardening. I was amazed by how many crazy varieties of vegetables you could grow that just weren't available at the supermarket. Harvesting vegetables that I've grown and nurtured from seed still brings me so much joy to this day. There's something even more magical about harvesting a crop when it's purple, spiky or a little funny looking! These weird and wonderful crops spark curiosity and remind me that gardening isn't just practical, it's playful too!

OCA

These small tubers taste like lemony potatoes. They also have delicious lemon-flavoured edible leaves.

1 Order tubers online. Plant into large pots in spring, 5cm deep.

2 Keep on top of watering.

3 Harvest the tubers after the leaves have been killed by frost.

CHIOGGIA BEETROOT

This Italian heirloom variety has pink and white candy-striped rings in the centre.

1 Sow seeds any time from mid-spring to mid-summer.

2 Sow direct into the ground, 2.5cm deep, 10cm apart.

3 Cover the seeds and water.

4 Water during dry spells, harvest once the beetroots are golf-ball-sized or larger.

MASHUA

Similar to radishes, these tubers taste peppery and have beautiful edible leaves and orange-yellow flowers. They are related to nasturtiums.

1 Order tubers online and plant into large pots or in the ground after last frost, 5cm deep.

2 Give the leaves something to climb up – they can grow up to 3m tall.

3 Harvest leaves for salads throughout the season and harvest tubers in late autumn.

PURPLE CARROTS

The delicious carrot flavour we all know and love, just in a fun colour!

1 Sow carrot seeds any time between April and July.

2 Prep the area by removing all weeds and making sure the ground isn't full of large stones, as these will make the carrots fork. Make a shallow drill 1cm deep. Water it and sprinkle seeds thinly along it, then cover them over.

3 Once the seedlings have grown 5–10cm tall, thin them by removing excess seedlings so the remaining plants are 5–8cm apart.

4 They'll be ready to harvest 12–16 weeks after sowing.

RAINBOW TOMATOES

There are hundreds of varieties of tomatoes that come in all different colours, shapes and patterns.

1 Sow the seeds into small pots or seed trays, eight weeks before your last frost date.

2 Keep indoors on a sunny windowsill until all risk of frost has passed.

3 Harden off, then plant outside or in greenhouse or polytunnel, and support with a bamboo cane.

4 Water deeply every few days in dry spells.

5 Harvest as soon as the fruits are ripe.

WHITE CUCUMBERS

These aren't your standard green cucumbers…

1 Sow seeds into small pots indoors in late spring, about four weeks before your last frost.

2 Plant out once all risk of frost has passed, ideally giving them something to climb up.

3 Water generously.

4 Keep on top of harvesting – one plant could give you up to twenty cucumbers.

5

6

7

10

CRAFT A SWEET PEA TEEPEE

I absolutely love sweet pea teepees. In fact, I love pretty much any structure that's covered in flowers (see my 'Secret Garden' archway on page 48). The great thing about this floral teepee is that you can leave an opening in the front that's big enough for you to crawl into and sit in the centre. This way, you can completely surround yourself with flowers, making the perfect place to sit outside and connect with nature. It's a simple but extremely effective project.

WHAT YOU'LL NEED

Seven 9cm plant pots
Peat-free multipurpose compost
Sweet pea seeds
A sunny, weed free area of the garden, at least 1m^2
Bamboo canes or other large sticks at least 2m long
String
Scissors

WHEN TO START
Early spring

WHEN TO ENJOY
Summer

1. Fill your 9cm plant pots with compost and poke in three seeds per pot.

2. Water and place on a sunny windowsill inside. Continue watering when the top 2cm of compost feels dry when you poke your finger in.

3. Once all risk of frost has passed, make your teepee by pushing bamboo canes into the prepared ground in a circle, leaving an opening at the front.

4. Secure them together at the top with string.

5. Tie rings of string horizontally around the bamboo canes to give your plants plenty to cling onto. Remember to leave the front of the teepee open.

6. Plant your sweet pea seedlings in the ground at the base of your teepee, adding plenty of compost into each planting hole for extra soil fertility.

7. As the sweet peas grow, they may need some help to cling onto the structure, so secure them loosely with string. The plants should soon find their own way and scramble up without any extra help.

8. Water regularly in dry spells.

9. As your plants begin to bloom, you could either cut the flowers and bring them indoors to enjoy or leave them on the plants and enjoy them outside. Just cut them off as they go past their best, as this will encourage them to continue blooming.

10. Remember to take the time to sit under your teepee, maybe to read a book or even meditate.

GROW YOUR OWN PLANT POTS

If you've had a flick through the projects in this book, it'll come as no surprise to you that I'm a little bit obsessed with growing mushrooms (see pages 165 and 174). It's such a fun and interesting process that involves a little bit of patience and just a dash of science. In this project, you'll learn how to make your own plant pots using mycelium – which is sort of the root-like structure of mushrooms, a network of tiny white threads that usually grow underground or inside dead wood. These plant pots are fully compostable so they could either be planted straight into the ground with the plant still inside them, or added to your compost bin.

WHAT YOU'LL NEED
Rubbing alcohol
Two plastic plant pots to use as moulds (about 15cm, or three smaller pots)
Large bowl
300g hardwood pellets
500ml room temperature water
75g flour
250g grey oyster mushroom spawn
Baking paper
Large cardboard box
Baking tray large enough to fit your two plant pots

WHEN TO START
This project can be done year-round, but I often do it in spring to make pots to grow my spring plants in

WHEN TO ENJOY
Year-round

1 Clean your hands and all work surfaces. Sterilize your plant pots by wiping them with rubbing alcohol and leaving to dry.

2 Put your wood pellets in a bowl and add the water to rehydrate them, then mix in the flour and mushroom spawn.

3 Line your plant pots with baking paper, then add the wood pellet mixture to them, pressing it against the sides and bottom of the pots to create an even layer about 1cm thick.

4 Add another layer of baking paper over the top of the pots to help keep moisture in, then put the pots inside the cardboard box and store in a dark place in your house for the mycelium to grow.

5 After about five days, the mycelium should have colonized the plant pots – you'll know if it's worked if you see a layer of white fluffy mycelium covering the surface of the pots. Remove the top layer of baking paper, then carefully remove the mycelium plant pots from their moulds.

6 Place them on a baking tray, and then put them back into the cardboard box for a further three days.

7 After three days, the mycelium should have fully colonized the wood pellet mixture. Remove the pots from the cardboard box and place in a preheated oven at 140°C for 45 minutes.

8 Remove from the oven and leave to cool completely. Plant up your mycelium plant pots.

2

2

3

8

7

SOW EDIBLE FLOWERS

One surefire way to make every meal joyful is to cover it in edible flowers. When I first started garnishing my meals with edible flowers I felt like I'd unlocked a cheat code to fancy food. Every meal looks like so much more love and care has gone into it, just with the simple addition of a few pretty flowers. Even if I'm making myself a speedy dinner, I'll still garnish it with a few chive blossoms or calendula petals. It's such a quick and simple act of self-care but it really goes a long way.

CALENDULA

This medicinal plant comes in colours that range from orange and yellow, to pink and peach. It readily self seeds (more plants will come up next year).

Sow indoors from seed in early spring and plant out after the last frost for early blooms, or sow direct where you'd like them to flower after last frost.

CHIVE

Purple flowers that taste like onion or garlic. They are perennial (come back every year).

Grow from seed in spring and then divide the plants year after year.

VIOLA

These beautiful flowers are often used in restaurants and are great for displaying on cakes and desserts.

Readily available from garden centres and supermarkets as small plants, or grow from seed indoors in spring and plant out after the last frost.

NASTURTIUM

This plant readily self-seeds and can act as a trap crop or companion plant. It's edible leaves and flowers come in shades of red, yellow, orange, cream and pink.

Sow indoors in early spring and plant out after the last frost for early blooms, or sow direct where you'd like them to flower after the last frost.

CORNFLOWER

Loved by pollinators, these pretty flowers come in shades of blue, purple, pink and white. They also make great cut flowers.

Direct sow in spring into the ground where you'd like them to flower.

BORAGE

Another plant that readily self-seeds, borage's blue star-shaped flowers have a cucumber flavour that's great in drinks, salads and desserts.

Sow indoors in early spring and plant out after the last frost.

CRAFT MINDFUL SMUDGE STICKS

These bundles of herbs have been used for centuries to cleanse spaces, objects and people of negative energy. Smudge sticks have roots in Indigenous cultures across the Americas, and this project has been inspired by these rituals to bring mindfulness and intention into your daily life. The act of growing, harvesting and crafting your own smudge stick is an invitation to slow down and connect with the seasons.

WHAT YOU'LL NEED
Young smudge stick plants (see below for suggestions)
A large pot to plant into
Free-draining compost
Cotton string
Scissors

WHEN TO START
Spring

WHEN TO ENJOY
Enjoy your dried smudge sticks year-round

1. Select your desired plants from the list below, and plant in full sun into pots filled with free-draining compost (you could plant these into the ground instead if you have a suitable growing space).

2. Keep on top of watering your plants during dry periods and once they're large enough you can start to harvest them.

3. Cut 15cm long stems off your plants and bundle together – you could create bundles from individual plants or mix them together to create more visual interest and to combine the properties of each plant. Don't make your bundles too thick as they need to be able to dry out fully – slightly wider than thumb thickness is ideal.

4. Tightly wrap your bundles with cotton string from bottom to top, tying it off firmly.

5. Hang your smudge sticks to dry in a dark, dry, and well ventilated area for up to four weeks. They should feel dry and crispy to the touch when they're ready. Don't rush this step, you need to make sure the sticks are fully dry to be able to store and burn them.

6. Once fully dry, your smudge sticks are ready to use! Use them with intention when you need to clear your mind or space of negative energy. To use, light the end of the smudge stick and allow to burn for 20 seconds, then blow out the flame. Slowly walk around your space with the smudge stick to allow the smoke to waft around. To extinguish, press into a fireproof bowl.

SMUDGE STICK PLANTS

Sage
Cleanses and purifies spaces, objects and people

Lavender
Helps with relaxation, clear thinking and focus

Mugwort
Can induce vivid dreams

Rosemary
Purifies spaces, promotes mental clarity

Thyme
Helps remove negativity with emotional healing

3

4

6

PLANT A SHADE GARDEN

We've all got those dark, dingy corners of our garden and it can be quite tricky to know what to do with them. Luckily, there are actually plenty of plants that thrive in these conditions – you just need to check you're planting the right plant in the right place. This project will help you transform the gloomiest areas of your garden into thriving havens full of life and beautiful plants.

WHAT YOU'LL NEED
A selection of plants that thrive in full or partial shade
A shady or partially shaded area of your garden
Peat-free multipurpose or homemade compost

WHEN TO START
Spring, after last frost

WHEN TO ENJOY
Year-round

1 Select your shade-loving plants (see suggestions below).

2 Prepare the shady planting area by removing all weeds and adding a good top dressing of compost.

3 Lay your plants out (still in their pots) and arrange them until you're happy with the configuration, making sure you give them enough space to grow to their full size.

4 Remove from the pots and plant into your shady garden bed.

5 Water in and keep on top of watering during dry periods.

SHADE-LOVING PLANTS
Foxgloves
Ferns
Hostas
Hellebores
Sweet woodruff
Astilbe
Pulmonaria
Bluebells
Snowdrops
Bellflower
Aquilegia

TIP: You could also create a shaded pot if you don't have in-ground growing space.

SUMMER

Summer is the season of abundance. The long days give us so much more time to spend outdoors, especially if the weather is kind. This is the season when many plants are at their best – herbs are luscious, berries are plump and juicy, and flowers are blooming beautifully. This bountiful time gives us so many creative ways to use what's growing. Summer feels like such a celebration to me – I love to use this time of year to really have fun with gardening and make the most of the extra daylight hours by spending as much time outdoors as possible.

MAKE HERBAL LIP BALM

Crafting your own lip balm using the plants from your garden is a lovely way to carry a piece of your garden in your pocket. The act of transforming your plants into a useful item is extremely rewarding. I love that this is a hands-on project which harnesses the healing properties of plants in your garden. There are a variety of homegrown herbs and flowers you could infuse in these lip balms, for example lavender, mint and rose petals, but I've opted for calendula flowers due to their skin-healing properties.

WHAT YOU'LL NEED
1½ tbsp dried calendula flowers (or edible, skin-safe flowers/herbs of choice)
Small jar with lid
4 tsp carrier oil such as sweet almond oil, jojoba oil or extra virgin olive oil
Muslin or sieve
Heatproof bowl (to fit the saucepan, creating a double boiler)
1 tsp beeswax or soy wax
3 drops organic essential oil (skin safe, e.g. orange or lavender – optional)
Three 10ml lip balm containers

WHEN TO START
Summer

WHEN TO ENJOY
Year-round

1 Add your calendula flowers (or flowers/herbs of choice) to a small jar and cover with your carrier oil. Screw the lid on the jar and leave to infuse in a dark place for two weeks, shaking every couple of days to ensure the flowers are covered in the oil and are infusing nicely. After two weeks, strain the oil by pouring it through a muslin or sieve. Collect the oil and discard the flowers.

2 Add an inch or two of water to a saucepan and bring to a simmer.

3 Add the infused oil and the wax to a heatproof bowl and place this on top of your pan of simmering water.

4 Once the wax is completely melted, turn the heat off and add your essential oils (if using).

5 Give everything a good stir and pour into your lip balm containers.

6 Once your lip balms have cooled and set, they're ready to use.

BLEND YOUR OWN BOTANICAL BATH SOAKS

Taking a long, relaxing bath can be just the reset you need after a stressful day. I've always loved indulging in bath products as a treat — soaking in them feels like a nice little act of self-care. These homemade bath soaks feel even more special. Crafting them yourself, and knowing every single ingredient in them and its purpose, makes them feel even more luxurious.

Each herb you add has its own benefits, from soothing the skin to calming the mind, so you can make a unique blend that's tailored to what you need and the scents you love. These also make thoughtful gifts for anyone in your life who might need a little extra relaxation. The best part is, they're *so* easy to make!

WHAT YOU'LL NEED
A total of 3 cups of any combination of the dried herbs and flowers listed opposite
Five unprinted 100% cotton drawstring bags (about 10 x 15cm)

WHEN TO START
Summer

WHEN TO ENJOY
Year-round

1 Add your chosen dried herbs and flowers to a large bowl and mix with your hands until evenly dispersed.

2 Fill each cotton bag with the dried herb and flower mixture and tie the drawstring to close.

3 To use, tie one bag to your hot water tap as you run a bath, or simply place the whole bag in your bath like a giant, soothing teabag. Use whenever you need some relaxation and self-care.

CREATE YOUR PERFECT BLEND

Calendula flowers
Soothe irritated skin, aid minor wound healing, can help treat skin conditions such as eczema, antifungal and antimicrobial.

Meadowsweet flowers
Anti-inflammatory, these calm inflamed skin and acne, and can help with joint pain.

Mint leaves
Cooling and soothes tired muscles, relieves tension and stress.

Chamomile flowers
Promote relaxation and improve sleep quality, soothe irritated skin and can help treat conditions such as eczema. Can also help relieve muscle pain.

Rose petals
Scent helps to reduce stress and anxiety, can reduce redness and comfort irritation. They also help to treat skin conditions such as eczema.

Lavender
Promotes relaxation and improves sleep quality. It may also alleviate anxiety and depression, is anti-inflammatory and can help treat acne.

Lemon balm leaves
Can help relieve anxiety, and improve sleep. Also helps treat acne, bites, stings, cuts and grazes.

Mullein leaves
Anti-inflammatory, can help soothe skin irritation and aches.

1

1

3

MAKE HOMEGROWN FIZZY DRINKS

These fizzy drinks are naturally fermented using a ginger bug. Just like gardening, fermentation is all about nurturing living cultures that transform simple ingredients into something thriving and beneficial. Both practices give you the satisfaction of watching something you've cared for come to life. There's strong scientific evidence linking gut health to mental wellbeing. The probiotics from fermented food and drinks help to support a healthy gut microbiome, which can influence mood, energy levels and mental wellbeing. These refreshing drinks can be customized by adding whatever flavours you enjoy, and are wonderful when made with seasonal, homegrown and foraged fruits.

WHAT YOU'LL NEED
Organic fresh ginger, grated
Raw sugar
Filtered water
Jar
Tea towel
Clip-top bottles
800ml fruit juice of your choice (homegrown or store-bought)

WHEN TO START
These can be made at any time of year, but I love to make them in summer when the garden is full of berries

WHEN TO ENJOY
Year-round

1 Make a ginger bug by adding 1 tablespoon of ginger, 3 teaspoons of sugar and 3 tablespoons of filtered water to a jar and stirring until the sugar has dissolved.

2 Cover the jar with a tea towel and leave for 24 hours, stirring every few hours or whenever you walk past it.

3 Feed your ginger bug daily by adding one tablespoon ginger, 1 teaspoon sugar and a splash of water. After a few days, you should see bubbles start to form on the surface – this is a sign that your ginger bug is active and ready to use.

4 To make a soda, combine 60ml ginger bug starter with 800ml fruit juice and 1 tablespoon of sugar.

5 Bottle and leave at room temperature for 3–5 days. Remember to 'burp' the bottles daily – which means opening and closing the bottles to avoid a build-up of carbonation.

6 Once they're bubbly, they're ready to drink.

MAKE LAVENDER SLEEP POUCHES

When you think of relaxation, chances are one of the first plants that comes to mind is lavender. It's thought to have been introduced to the UK by the Romans nearly 2,000 years ago, who may have used it to dress wounds, repel insects and even bathe with, as an early form of aromatherapy.

Today, there is plenty of research to suggest that breathing in the heady scent of lavender can improve sleep quality – and getting a good night's sleep is essential for supporting mental and physical health. Poor sleep has been linked to increased levels of stress and anxiety, so incorporating relaxing plants like lavender into your bedtime routine can be a simple but powerful step towards improving your wellbeing.

These lavender sleep pouches are easy to make and utilize scraps of fabric you might have lying around.

WHAT YOU'LL NEED
Lavender stems
String
Scissors
White rice
Scraps of fabric
Plate to use as template (about 20cm diameter)
Pen
Ribbon (optional)
Tablespoon

WHEN TO START
Early summer, just before the lavender flowers fully open

WHEN TO ENJOY
Year-round

1 Harvest your lavender when the flower buds have developed their colour but haven't fully opened yet. Cut a few inches below the flower bud, including some leaves for extra fragrance.

2 Tie your lavender stems in small bunches with string and hang to dry upside down somewhere cool, dark and well ventilated for 2–4 weeks. (To make your own herb dryer for this step, see page 162.)

3 Once dry, pluck the lavender buds and leaves off their stalks and discard the stalks (to avoid having sharp or bulky bits in your pouches).

4 Combine your lavender flowers and leaves with white rice in a bowl – I use one part rice to two parts lavender. The rice helps to hold the scent and adds weight.

5 Lay your scrap fabric flat, place your plate on top of the fabric and draw around it.

6 Cut out circles from the fabric to make as many pouches as you'd like.

7 Place a couple of tablespoons of your lavender and rice mixture in the centre of each fabric circle, then gather the material to make a little pouch around the lavender.

8 Tie the neck of the pouch with ribbon or string.

TO USE: Place a lavender pouch by your bedside and gently squeeze it before bed to release the scent and help you unwind. You could also place your lavender pouches in drawers or wardrobes to keep clothes smelling fresh and repel moths.

4

4

7

8

8

PLANT A HERBAL TEA GARDEN

There are so many easy-to-grow plants that have amazing benefits for your physical and mental health, and one of the easiest ways to reap the benefits is to make them into a herbal tea. From calming chamomile to uplifting lemon balm, growing your own herbal tea plants turns making a simple cup of tea into a self-care ritual. My favourite thing about growing my own tea garden is that I can make my own blends, mixing complementary flavours or plants that give the benefits I need that day.

WHAT YOU'LL NEED
Herbal tea plants (see suggestions below)
A sunny area of garden or large container to plant into

WHEN TO START
Early summer

WHEN TO ENJOY
Year-round

1 Choose your herbal tea plants. Many of the herbs I've listed below are widely available as small plants from garden centres. Plants like calendula, borage and chamomile are easy and cheap to grow from seed (see page 28 for how to grow chamomile from a teabag).

2 Find a sunny spot for your herbal tea garden. This could be in a large container or in a garden bed – just make sure the area is free from weeds and has free-draining soil.

3 Remove your plants from their pots and plant into the prepared area, making sure to leave plenty of space for each plant to grow.

4 Water thoroughly, and continue to water every few days during dry spells.

5 Harvest your herbs as and when you fancy a fresh cup of herbal tea, and steep in hot water.

6 Make sure to dry some of your harvest (see page 162 for DIY herb dryer) to use in the winter.

HERBAL TEA PLANTS

Borage
Reduces inflammation, improves skin health

Mint
Cooling, aids digestion, relieves headaches and congestion

Calendula
Promotes skin health, anti-inflammatory, supports digestion

Lavender
Aids relaxation, reduces stress, improves sleep

Lemon balm
Uplifting, eases anxiety

Lemon verbena
Calming, helps digestion, reduces anxiety

Fennel
Aids digestion, relieves period pain, reduces bloating

Echinacea
Boosts immune system, helps fight against colds and flu

Sage
Helps ease menopausal symptoms including hot flashes and night sweats

Chamomile
Calming, helps with sleep and digestion

TEA BLEND IDEAS

MOOD-BOOSTING TEA

6–8 fresh lemon balm leaves
6–8 fresh mint leaves
3 calendula flowers

Steep in hot (not boiling) water for 5 minutes and enjoy. This would also work well poured over ice on a hot day.

RELAXING TEA

8 fresh chamomile flower heads
2 fresh lavender flower buds
5 fresh lemon verbena leaves

Steep in hot (not boiling) water for 5 minutes in the evening and sip slowly to wind down.

SOOTHING DIGESTIVE TEA

5 fresh lemon verbena leaves
1 tbsp chopped fresh fennel fronds
2 fresh lavender flower buds

Steep in hot (not boiling) water for 6–7 minutes and enjoy the soothing effects.

CREATE A CONTAINER POND

Ponds play a crucial role in supporting biodiversity, and the great news is that even small ponds can make a huge difference. This project shows you how to upcycle disused containers into wildlife havens. Creating a pond doesn't have to be complicated, expensive or take up a lot of room; something small and simple can become a vital refuge for a wide variety of creatures. It's amazing how much life can appear once your pond is in place. Watching it flourish is incredibly rewarding, as you see the impact your little homemade oasis has on the local ecosystem.

WHAT YOU'LL NEED
Waterproof container
Pond liner (optional)
Gravel or small stones
Larger rocks and branches
A few aquatic plants (from a local garden centre or online)

WHEN TO START
Early summer, before the weather heats up

WHEN TO ENJOY
Year-round

1 Choose your container. It needs to be sturdy and hold water without leaking, like an old sink, wooden barrel or metal trough.

2 Choose a location for your pond. It's best to put it in a spot that gets about 3–6 hours of sun a day – sun is essential for plants and wildlife but too much can cause algae growth. Place your container in its final position, as it will be heavy once full. Container ponds look lovely when they've been sunk into the ground, but the wildlife will be just as happy with one placed above ground if they have a way in and out.

3 Prepare your container by blocking any drainage holes or lining with a pond liner. Clean the container thoroughly to remove any dirt or possible chemicals that could harm the wildlife.

4 Add a layer of gravel to the bottom of your container, which helps to anchor plants and creates habitat for beneficial microbes.

5 Next, add large stones and branches to your container to create a stairway for creatures. Repeat on the outside if your pond is above ground.

6 Fill your container with water. Rainwater is ideal for this, but if you need to use tap water, just leave it for 24 hours for the chlorine to evaporate.

7 Add your aquatic plants. You can use a mix of submerged, floating and marginal plants. These are great to add as they help oxygenate the water and provide habitat for little creatures. Pondweed is great for keeping the water clear.

8 Maintain your pond by topping up water in dry spells and removing any dead plant material.

9 Take time to watch and observe your little oasis come to life.

DYE CLOTHES AND MATERIAL WITH PLANTS

Turn drab materials into items that spark joy by dying them with the plants you've lovingly grown in your garden. You'd be surprised how many plants in your local area will make beautiful dyes. It can be fun to experiment with different plants to see what colours you get. You could even try tie-dyeing. The colours aren't always what you'd expect either. The shades and tones can vary depending on the time of year you collect the plants and the mordant you use. Mordant is a substance used to treat fabric before dyeing it to help the colour fix and prevent fading. Aluminium salts (also known as alum) are most common and can easily be ordered online at low cost.

WHAT YOU'LL NEED

Mordant – alum works best to get brighter colours, but you could try soy milk or vinegar if you want to use what you already have in your kitchen (optional)

A large heatproof pot/saucepan – big enough to fit the fabric you're dyeing in, with plenty of room around it

Scissors

Dye plants – collect a substantial amount of your chosen dye plant (at least 25 per cent of the weight of the fabric). Fresher leaves and flowers generally produce more vibrant colours, but older plants will still give you interesting hues

Clean fabric – natural fibres like cotton, linen or wool work best

Strainer

Rubber gloves

WHEN TO START

Summer is when most plants are abundantly available, but this is an 'evergreen' project which depends on the plant dyes you intend to use

WHEN TO ENJOY

Straightaway

DYE PLANTS AND THEIR COLOURS

Chamomile
Pale yellow

Marigolds
Sunny yellow

Nettles
Pale green

Elderberries
Purple

Avocado pits and skins
Pink

Acorns
Brown

Onion skins
Orange

MARIGOLD

AVOCADO

NETTLE

CHAMOMILE

2

4

4

5

1 First, prepare the mordant (if using). For alum, dissolve 10g of alum per litre of water, making sure you have enough water to cover the fabric once it's in the pot. Put the water into the pot over a medium heat and bring the water to a simmer. Add the fabric to the solution and reduce the heat to a medium-low. Soak for an hour, then rinse. For vinegar, soak the fabric in a one part vinegar to four parts water solution for an hour, then rinse. For soy milk, mix one part soy milk with five parts water, then soak your fabric in this solution for 24 hours. Remove the fabric, wring out excess water, then leave to air dry completely. The pot can now be emptied.

2 Chop your plant material into small pieces, about 1cm in size, then add to the pot and cover with water. The more plant material you add, the stronger the resulting colour will be.

3 Bring to a simmer, then reduce the heat to low and leave to infuse for an hour. Strain out your plant material to leave you with a clear dye bath.

4 Place your fabric into the dye bath and soak on a low heat for an hour, stirring occasionally to ensure you get an even colour. Make sure the liquid doesn't boil. To get an even deeper shade, take the dye bath off the heat and leave the fabric to soak in the liquid overnight.

5 Remove the fabric from the dye bath and rinse it thoroughly in cold water until the water runs clear. Hang to dry out of direct sunlight, as UV light can cause the colours to fade.

TIP: To prolong the life of your naturally dyed fabrics, handwash them in cold water with a gentle detergent rather than putting them in the washing machine.

GROW YOUR OWN SALAD BAR

Growing my own food was the thing that really got me hooked on gardening. It's one thing planting seeds, nurturing them and watching them grow into beautiful healthy plants, but being able to *eat* what you've grown adds a whole new level of satisfaction. When beginner gardeners ask me what crop to start with, my answer is always salad. Easy to grow, it rewards you with seemingly endless harvests and it's a huge money saver if you often buy bagged salad. Salad is also a great place to start when it comes to veggie gardening as you can grow it year-round — just check the seed packets to see if each crop is suitable for the season you'd like to grow it in.

WHAT YOU'LL NEED

A area of garden or container to plant into
Peat-free multipurpose or homemade compost
Lettuce, mizuna or rocket seeds
Radish seeds
Spring onion seeds
Nasturtium and/or calendula seeds

WHEN TO START

Any time of year outside extreme temperatures — seeds won't germinate if temperatures are too hot or too cold

WHEN TO ENJOY

Year-round

1 Choose where to locate your salad bar. Most salad plants thrive in full sun, however some dappled shade can help prevent plants bolting in the height of summer.

2 Prepare the area by removing large weeds (remember that some weeds like dandelions are edible, so they can be left to add into salads), and mulch with a layer of compost. If planting in a container, fill just below the top with compost.

3 Water the area and start sowing.

4 For lettuce, mizuna and rocket seeds, make drills about 1cm deep with the side of your hand, sprinkle the seeds thinly along the bottom of the drill and cover it with compost. Space each drill about 25cm apart.

5 Sow radish seeds in between your rows of salad. I once again make a drill 1cm deep in the soil and sow each seed about 2cm apart. Cover the seeds back over — these will be ready to harvest in about four weeks. Sow more seeds every couple of weeks for continuous harvests.

6 Sow spring onions around the outside of the bed or container, as their strong scent helps to deter pests and protect the other plants. Sow these in the same way as the lettuce seeds.

7 For nasturtium or calendula seeds, poke the seeds into the soil about 2cm deep and 15cm apart — these plants are larger. Nasturtium leaves and flowers, and calendula's sunny flowers, can all be added to salads and both plants are a hit with pollinators.

8 Make sure to water frequently, especially during dry spells.

9 Start harvesting the salad leaves as soon as each plant has a few leaves that are about 10cm long, by picking individual leaves. This allows the plant to continue growing and produce more leaves. Harvest the radishes from about four weeks after sowing — you may see them peeking out the top of the soil. Harvest the spring onions from about eight weeks, and nasturtium and calendula flowers as soon as they bloom.

MAKE AN OLLA INSECT BATH

Ollas are terracotta pots that are buried in the soil to aid irrigation – there's evidence to suggest ollas have been used in this way for thousands of years. They're simple to create and so effective – just fill them with water every few days and the water slowly seeps into the surrounding soil, delivering moisture straight to plant roots. Unlike surface watering, which often evaporates quickly, especially in the summer, ollas direct the water underground where it's needed most.

Ollas can do much more than just water your plants, though. With the addition of a shallow water dish on top, you can turn them into a mini oasis for wildlife. Insects often struggle to find water during the dry months, so creating a little drinking station for them can make a huge difference. It won't take long for bees, butterflies and other insects to find it, and it's so rewarding to watch wildlife thrive thanks to something you've made.

WHAT YOU'LL NEED
20cm terracotta plant pot (unglazed)
Mounting or moldable putty
20cm plant pot saucer
Stones and rocks in various different sizes

WHEN TO START
Summer

WHEN TO ENJOY
Summer and during dry spells

1 Your plant pot will most likely have a drainage hole in the bottom, so plug this using your mounting putty or moldable putty to make it watertight.

2 Dig a hole in the ground where you want to place your olla. It's best to locate this close to plants' roots – either near a large plant, or you could plant a ring of smaller plants around it. Place it so that about 1cm of your pot pokes above the soil surface level, this makes refilling easier and keeps soil out.

3 Fill the pot with water and place the saucer on top.

4 Arrange your stones and rocks on the saucer, leaving some that poke above the water surface (once filled) so that insects can land and anything that falls in can climb out.

5 Add a few rocks around the outside of the pot too, to create access for crawling insects.

6 Fill the saucer with water.

7 Remember to check up on the olla and saucer every few days and keep topping them up with water as needed.

TRANSFORM FABRICS WITH FLOWER HAMMERING

The first time I tried flower hammering, my mind was blown. Who knew something so beautiful could be so simple? This project is a great way to capture the beauty of summer to enjoy year-round. It's a lovely way to upcycle clothes or fabric that needs a new lease of life. I've always wanted to try flower hammering on bedding or a large tablecloth, but I haven't yet found the time (or quantity of flowers) needed to undertake such a large project. For now, I'll stick to smaller scale items such as t-shirts, tote bags and tea towels, which look just as pretty.

WHAT YOU'LL NEED
Flowers and/or leaves
Chopping board
Clean fabric – natural fibres like cotton or linen work best
Baking paper
Hammer or mallet
Clean tea towel or cloth
Iron

WHEN TO START
Summer, or whenever you have access to lots of fresh blooming flowers

WHEN TO ENJOY
Year-round

1 Select your flowers or leaves. Vivid colours and thin petals and leaves work best, but it can be so much fun to experiment with different plants. Thick, juicy flowers may bleed out a bit too much when you hammer them, so bear that in mind.

2 Place your chopping board on the table to protect it from the hammering and the flower dyes.

3 Arrange the flowers across your fabric, placing them face down. You could arrange them all at once so you know how your final item will look or add them one by one.

4 Lay a piece of baking paper over the flowers and use your hammer to tap firmly and evenly across each flower. For larger flowers, start in the centre and work your way to the outside, making sure you've covered the whole area.

5 Once you've finished hammering, lift the baking paper and peel away the flowers and leaves from your fabric, you should now see colourful imprints on your fabric.

6 To set the design, place a tea towel or cloth over your item and iron on a low heat.

3

4

5

PLANTS FOR YOUR HERBAL PATHWAY

Lavender
Great for relaxation, plus its pretty purple flowers are a hit with bees

Lemon balm
Plant for its bright citrusy fragrance that lifts mood and can ease anxiety

Chamomile
This plant's soothing scent can help with relaxation and sleep, and looks lovely spilling over the edges of the path

Mint
Offers a refreshing and energizing aroma that helps to lift mood

Thyme
An excellent choice for its uplifting and cleansing fragrance

Sage
With a grounding earthy scent, sage is often associated with cleansing and purification

PLANT A HERBAL PATHWAY

There's something so grounding about walking through a pathway of herbs: as you brush past them, each plant emits a soothing scent. They're also an invitation to slow down and a lovely way to connect with your senses. If you'd like to create one, you could plant herbs either side of a garden path that you walk down often, or even tuck them between stepping stones. This is another customizable project that allows you to choose the plants that work for you — the options are endless. For a bold look with a relaxing scent, you could plant a full pathway of lavender, while a tapestry of plants like chamomile, lemon balm and mint would offer a beautiful bouquet of soothing and uplifting scents.

WHAT YOU'LL NEED
An area of your garden you walk past often
Your chosen herb plants (quantity will vary depending on the size of your space; see opposite)
Compost
Bottomless plant pots for mint and lemon balm (to stop it taking over – optional)
Horticultural grit and/or compost (optional)

WHEN TO START
Early summer

WHEN TO ENJOY
Straightaway

1 Choose a location for your herbal pathway. Opt for an area you walk past often, ideally in a sunny spot if your chosen herbs like to grow in full sun.

2 Choose your herbs (see opposite).

3 Prepare the soil — Mediterranean herbs like lavender, thyme and sage require good drainage, so you may need to work some horticultural grit into the soil. Plants like lemon balm, mint and chamomile need more moisture to thrive, so you may need to add some extra good-quality compost to improve moisture retention.

4 Mint and lemon balm can be real thugs in the garden, if you want to avoid them taking over the rest of the area, plant them in bottomless pots so that they don't spread too much.

5 Plant your herbs into the prepared area, making sure the crown of the plant (where the plant meets the roots) is level with the rest of the soil. Plant them close to the edges of the path so they emit their scent as you brush past.

6 Water in, and keep on top of watering during dry spells.

7 Enjoy your herbal pathway by running your hands over the leaves or simply brushing past and breathing in the scents.

GROW YOUR OWN CHRISTMAS DINNER

It may seem crazy to utter the 'C word' in summer (I am, of course, talking about the word 'Christmas') but if you want to harvest any vegetables during the winter months, it's important to get them started early – this is because daylight hours get much shorter in the winter which slows plant growth. Growing your own Christmas dinner is very satisfying! It feels like such an achievement to have grown even one element of such a special meal. If you don't celebrate Christmas, you can still use this as a guide for harvesting homegrown vegetables during the winter, and you can then use those veggies in whatever meal you fancy. I'd recommend inviting some friends or family around to celebrate your harvest. I've included instructions on how to grow Kalettes – a frillier, tastier version of Brussels sprouts. if you haven't tried these, I strongly recommend you give them a go.

WHAT YOU'LL NEED
Seeds for your favourite Christmas dinner plants
Garden beds and/or containers to plant into

WHEN TO START
Early summer

WHEN TO ENJOY
Christmas, or any other day in winter

CARROTS

Sow carrot seeds in early summer.

1. Make sure the area has loose, sandy soil, free from lots of large stones. You could plant them in a deep container if your garden has compacted soil.

2. Make a drill in the soil about 1cm deep, water it and sprinkle the seeds in thinly all the way along. If you are doing multiple rows, space each row about 30cm apart. Cover the drill with compost and give it another gentle water.

3. Carrot seeds need to be kept moist until germination, which can take up to two weeks. You can cover them with something like a plank of wood to keep in moisture, just make sure you keep checking on them and remove the plank once the seeds have started germinating.

4. Once the foliage is about 7cm tall, the carrots may need thinning – this is to give the roots plenty of space to swell to full size. Ideally, you should pull the smaller, thinner seedlings out and aim for a final spacing of 5cm apart.

5. Keep watered and weeded, and harvest for Christmas dinner.

PARSNIPS

Sow in late spring/early summer.

1. Prepare the soil as you did for the carrots.

2. Make a drill in the soil about 1cm deep, water it and sprinkle in the seeds all the way along. Parsnips can be very tricky to germinate. Make sure you buy fresh seeds and sow way more than you need. If doing multiple rows, space each row about 30cm apart. Cover the drill with compost and give it another gentle water.

3. Parsnip seeds need to be kept moist until germination, which can take 2–4 weeks. As with the carrots, cover them with a plank of wood to keep in moisture. Remove the plank once the seeds have started germinating.

4. Once the foliage is about 7cm tall, thin the parsnips out, so you're left with one every 15cm. Pull the smaller, thinner seedlings out.

5. Keep watered and weeded, and harvest for Christmas dinner.

POTATOES

Plant from midsummer onwards, 12 weeks before you want to harvest them.

1 Potato plants aren't frost hardy, so plant them in containers so you can put them somewhere sheltered when frost arrives – a cold frame, greenhouse or indoors will do. Use a big container that's at least 30cm wide with drainage holes in the bottom – you could even use an old compost bag and poke holes in the bottom for drainage.

2 Put a 15cm layer of compost in the bottom of the container, then add in two seed potatoes. If your container is larger, you can add more seed potatoes, just make sure they have plenty of space between them.

3 Cover the seed potatoes with another 15cm of compost and water them in.

4 As the foliage grows, keep adding layers of compost to almost completely cover it, until the pot is full.

5 Keep on top of watering and observe the weather forecast. Move somewhere sheltered when frost is due

6 The foliage may start to die down in autumn, which is normal. You can remove this and leave the potatoes in the pot until you're ready to harvest them.

BRUSSELS SPROUTS OR KALETTES

Sow in late spring/early summer.

1 Sow your Brussels sprout or Kalette seeds into modular seed trays filled with multipurpose or seed compost for the best protection against pests and diseases. Sow two seeds per cell and, after a few weeks, thin them out to one per cell, remove the smaller or weaker seedling. Water regularly.

2 Once the seedlings are about 10cm tall, they can be planted into their final position. Prepare the area by removing weeds and adding lots of good-quality compost.

3 Plant the seedlings at least 60cm apart and bury them up to the first set of leaves.

4 Cover with fine netting to prevent insect and bird damage (this is optional, but recommended).

5 Water regularly. You may also need to support the plants with a bamboo cane as they get taller, particularly if you're in a windy area.

6 Harvest your Brussels sprouts when they're about 2.5cm wide and firm but still closed, and harvest Kalettes when they're about 3cm wide.

CARROTS & PARSNIPS

POTATOES

KALETTES

PLANT A PIZZA OR PASTA GARDEN

Imagine walking into your garden and being able to harvest almost all the ingredients you need to make a pizza or pasta dish! Planting your own pizza or pasta garden is such a fun way to become even more connected with your food. Every ingredient tastes so much better when you've grown it yourself – from the fragrant scent of basil to the sweetness of sun-ripened tomatoes, each harvest will make you proud of your efforts. Planting tomatoes and herbs together make for easy harvesting, plus they make great companions for each other as the strong scent of the herbs helps to deter pests from the tomatoes. I've kept this project extra simple and achievable for beginner gardeners by including small shop-bought plants which are widely available from garden centres and even large supermarkets. If you'd like to save money or go the extra mile, you could grow the plants from seed instead – simply start these off indoors in early spring.

WHAT YOU'LL NEED
Your chosen pizza and pasta plants (see opposite)
A sunny area of the garden to plant into
Good-quality compost

WHEN TO START
Early summer (or early spring if growing from seed)

WHEN TO ENJOY
Mid to late summer

1 Choose your pizza or pasta plants (see opposite). Think about the recipes you like to make, then select the plants to make them. I recommend choosing a couple of herbs and combining them with one or two tomato plants, and other vegetables you fancy.

2 Find a sunny spot for your pizza or pasta plants.

3 Prepare the area by removing any vigorous weeds and adding in plenty of good-quality compost.

4 Plan the layout, making sure each plant has enough space to grow and plenty of light. Keep in mind the final heights of the plants – tomatoes tend to grow very tall (unless you've opted for a dwarf variety) so they could shade out anything growing behind them, they may also need to be supported with something like a bamboo cane as they grow.

5 Once you're happy with the layout, plant your herbs and veggies in their final growing position and give everything a good water.

6 Keep an eye on your pizza and pasta garden as it grows, and keep on top of watering during dry spells.

7 You can harvest your herbs as soon as the plants are a few inches tall by pinching out the stems just above a pair of leaves – this helps the plant to continue to grow nice and bushy.

8 Harvest tomatoes and peppers as soon as the fruits are ripe.

9 Harvest courgettes as soon as they're a few inches long.

10 Enjoy your homegrown harvests as part of a delicious pizza or bowl of pasta.

PLANTS FOR YOUR PIZZA OR PASTA GARDEN

Tomato
Basil
Oregano
Chilli
Sweet pepper
Courgette
Onions
Rocket
Spinach
Nasturtiums

PLANT A NIGHT SCENTED GARDEN

Often overlooked, moths play a vital role in our ecosystems. Many species help pollinate our plants, while their caterpillars provide an essential food source for bats and a variety of birds. Sadly, with light pollution on the rise and wild habitats shrinking, moth numbers are under threat. One of the simplest ways to help them is by creating a moth-friendly garden.

And the good news is, a moth garden is just as enjoyable for you as it is for them. Many of the flowers that moths love are beautifully scented, particularly in the evening – just when you might be winding down in the garden. Think of it as a nighttime pollinator patch, which connects you to the garden wildlife you might not see as often.

WHAT YOU'LL NEED
A sunny or part-shade spot
Compost
A mix of nectar-rich night scented plants (see box)
A shallow dish of water filled with pebbles for pollinators to land on

WHEN TO START
Late spring to early summer

WHEN TO ENJOY
Late spring to early autumn, particularly on warm sunny evenings

1 Choose a spot for your night scented garden. This could be an area where you enjoy sitting in the evenings. Part of the joy of this project is watching the moths visit at dusk and enjoying the scent of the flowers at sunset.

2 Weed the area and add compost to enrich the soil and keep your plants healthy.

3 Plant your scented flowers in clusters, then give everything a deep water.

4 Remember that moths also need plants for their caterpillars to eat. Different species eat different plants, so the best way to support them is to grow a diverse mix of trees, shrubs, flowers and even long grass if you can. The greener and more diverse your garden, the better it is for moths.

5 Avoid using pesticides and herbicides, as these can harm moths directly.

6 Put out a shallow dish of water filled with pebbles for pollinators to drink from.

7 Try to keep garden lights dim or switched off at night, as these can disorientate moths.

8 Sit peacefully at dusk, and watch your garden come alive in the most magical way.

MOTH-FRIENDLY PLANTS

Evening primrose
Nicotiana
Night scented stock
Honeysuckle
Jasmine
Valerian
Sweet rocket
Hemp-agrimony
Buddleja
Ivy

PROLONG SUMMER WITH A DIY FLOWER PRESS

Summer is such a beautiful season that's full of abundance. There are flowers blooming pretty much everywhere and, in the moment, it can be quite easy to forget how fleeting this season is. I love to preserve a little bit of the beauty of summer to look back on when I'm in the dark depths of winter. Pressed summer flowers are a great reminder of all the beauty that's to come, which is much needed on those drizzly winter and spring days when you feel like summer is never going to arrive.

WHAT YOU'LL NEED
Pencil
Two matching pieces of wood – I made mine 20 x 20cm (plywood or MDF work well)
A drill
At least four pieces of cardboard, cut smaller than the size of the wood
At least six pieces of plain paper, cut the same size as the cardboard
Flowers and leaves, for preserving
Four screws
Four washers and wing nuts

WHEN TO START
Summer, or whenever you have flowers and leaves you want to preserve

WHEN TO ENJOY
2–4 weeks later, once the flowers have dried

1 Mark where you're going to drill holes in the corners of both pieces of wood. I like to measure 2cm from the edge and draw lines all the way down each side. Drill holes in all four corners of one piece of wood, where the lines intersect.

2 Line up the two pieces of wood and make sure the holes you're about to make on the second piece of wood will match up with those in the first. Then drill holes in all four corners of the second piece of wood.

3 Assemble the flower press by placing the first piece of wood down, layering a piece of cardboard on top, followed by a piece of paper.

4 Collect flowers and leaves that you'd like to preserve, lay them out on top of the paper, making sure to space them apart so they don't overlap.

5 Lay a sheet of paper on top of your flowers, followed by a piece of cardboard. Continue layering cardboard, paper and flowers until the press is full or you've used up all the flowers you want to press. Make sure to finish with a piece of cardboard.

6 Place the second board on top, then thread the screws through the four holes on both pieces of wood. Thread washers and wing nuts onto the ends of the bolts, then tighten each one evenly to ensure even pressure.

7 Your flowers and leaves should be ready after 2–4 weeks. You can use them in craft projects or make yourself a book of pressed flowers to look through to remember what you've grown in your garden over the years. It's also nice to look back on in winter to remind you of sunnier times.

AUTUMN

The leaves starting to turn brown, the crisp frosty mornings and that special warm glowing light make autumn feel so magical. After the long days and abundance of summer, you may find yourself with lots of produce from the garden by autumn, so it's a great time of year to preserve what's grown so you can enjoy it all year round. As the days get shorter and shorter, I find myself bringing the garden indoors by starting projects that can be done within the house. Many people mourn for summer at this time of year, but I find autumn comforting. It's a season of slowing down, appreciating what we've harvested and gently preparing the garden (and ourselves) for a period of rest.

MAKE A WORM COMPOSTING BIN

The hardest workers in the garden by far, worms quietly turn decaying material into rich, fertile compost. By making a worm composting bin, you can harness their special talents into turning your food scraps – things that might otherwise end up in the bin – into markedly improved soil. If you grow your own food, this cycle feels even more satisfying. There's a real sense of reward in watching waste transform into something valuable – and every time you add scraps to the worm bin, you'll get a little reminder of the bigger cycle you're a part of. Plus, you get to say you're the proud owner of hundreds of slimy little pets (hopefully that doesn't put you off).

WHAT YOU'LL NEED
Two stackable storage boxes or buckets with one lid
A drill with 5mm drill bit
Bedding material e.g. shredded cardboard, old compost or coconut coir
Red wriggler worms (you can order these online)
Food scraps e.g. vegetable peelings, coffee grounds, teabags

WHEN TO START
Any time

WHEN TO ENJOY
Year-round

1 Decide where to locate your worm bin – a shed or sheltered area of the garden where it doesn't get too hot or too cold is ideal, as worms are most active between 13–27°C. You can keep a worm bin indoors, just don't add too much to it at once as it can produce odours.

2 Drill plenty of holes into the bottom of your top box for drainage, and a few on the sides for ventilation.

3 Place the top box (with holes) into the bottom box. This is to catch any liquid (or 'worm tea') that drains out.

4 Add a 10cm layer of damp but not soggy bedding material to the top box.

5 Place the worms on top of the bedding – they'll soon burrow down to escape the light.

6 Add a layer of food scraps on top of the bedding, no more than 8cm thick.

7 Cover the food scraps with another layer of bedding, this helps to decrease odours and prevent fruit flies.

8 Leave the worms to settle in for about a week and then start adding small amounts of food scraps, making sure to chop up any large items so the worms can break them down faster. Cover the food scraps with the same or additional bedding.

9 Once the wormery is full, you can harvest the compost. Worms usually congregate just below the food waste, so remove the top 20cm of the contents and set aside, ready to start the bin again. Harvest the remaining compost, and use it as a high-powered, nutrient-dense soil improver.

10 The water that gathers in the bottom bin can be used as a liquid fertilizer. To do so, dilute it at a rate of one part worm tea to ten parts water, and use around the garden.

PLANT EARLY FLOWERING BULBS

The colder months can often feel never-ending; it sometimes seems like spring will never arrive. During these dark and slightly gloomy days, it's a real blessing to have something to look forward to. Autumn is the perfect time to plant spring-flowering bulbs, giving them time to establish their root systems before the ground freezes. Many spring bulbs also require a period of cold to break dormancy, so planting in autumn will ensure that they bloom when spring finally comes around. I love the idea of tucking bulbs into the soil in the autumn so they can rest and prepare over winter – something I try to mirror in my own life. Some of the bulbs I've suggested in this project start blooming in late winter; they're a little bit of light at the end of a long dark tunnel, and a hint of the beauty that's on its way.

WHAT YOU'LL NEED
Your choice of spring flowering bulbs (see opposite)
Compost (if planting in pots or heavy soil)
Horticultural grit (optional)
A trowel or bulb planter

WHEN TO START
Autumn

WHEN TO ENJOY
Late winter to spring

1 Start by choosing your spring-flowering bulbs. I aim for a succession of blooms from January to summer, so there's always something flowering in my garden. Use the list (see opposite) as a guide to choosing bulbs that bloom through spring – this will vary depending on the variety and your climate.

2 Choose your spot: most bulbs thrive in a sunny position, however some (like bluebells and snowdrops) are happy in partial shade.

3 Amend your soil if needed. A lot of bulbs need well-draining soil to help them grow and prevent rotting. If you have heavy soil, dig in plenty of compost (and horticultural grit if you have it).

4 Scatter your bulbs where you want to plant them. For a natural look, you can gently throw the bulbs onto the ground and plant them where they land. Space them about 2–3 bulb-widths apart to give them plenty of room to grow. If planting in pots, you can plant them a bit closer together for an impactful display – I like to plant them so they're almost touching.

5 With your trowel or bulb planter, make small holes in the soil to plant each bulb into. A good, general rule is to plant bulbs at a depth of about three times the height of the bulb.

6 Cover the bulbs over and gently firm the soil down so the bulbs are nice and snug in their beds for winter. Water them in if the soil is dry.

7 Wait patiently for the beautiful blooms to appear in spring.

SPRING FLOWERING BULBS AND WHEN THEY BLOOM (DEPENDENT ON VARIETY)

Snowdrops
January to March

Crocus
January to March

Winter Aconite
January to March

Iris Reticulata
February to March

Daffodils
March to April

Hyacinths
March to April

Muscari/Grape Hyacinths
April to May

Tulips (best planted in early winter)
April to May

Bluebells
April to May

Alliums
May to June

PLANT A BULB LASAGNE

Bulb lasagnes, which get their name from being layered just like the Italian dish, are an amazing way of getting a whole season of blooms from just one pot. If you planted one type of bulb in each pot, it would only bloom for a month or two, leaving the rest of the year with only leaves, or sometimes nothing at all. But by layering a variety of early, mid-season and late-blooming flowers, you can enjoy colour from January right the way through to June. Perfect for gardeners who are short on space or anyone who wants to get maximum joy from every pot, bulb lasagnes are a lesson in making the most of what you have.

WHAT YOU'LL NEED
A selection of early, mid-season and late-blooming spring bulbs
A crock (broken piece of terracotta plant pot) or some large stones
A large pot (minimum 30cm wide and deep)
Peat-free multipurpose or homemade compost
Horticultural grit (optional)

WHEN TO START
Autumn

WHEN TO ENJOY
January to June

1 Select your bulbs. Choose three or more varieties that bloom at different times of the year, for example crocuses (January to March), daffodils (March to April), and Alliums (May to June). This ensures a succession of colour from late winter into early summer.

2 Place a crock or some large stones in the bottom of your plant pot to cover the drainage hole, this stops compost blocking it up but allows water to drain freely.

3 Add at least 15cm compost to the bottom of the plant pot. For the bottom layer of bulbs, you can go up to 25cm deep depending on the size of your pot and how many varieties you plan to layer. Mix in a couple of handfuls of horticultural grit if you have it, as this helps with drainage.

4 Place your largest and latest-flowering bulbs into the plant pot. This bottom layer of bulbs can be planted close together, so they are almost touching.

5 Cover them with a 5cm layer of compost, then place in your mid-season bulbs. Plant these slightly further apart, leaving a couple of centimetres between each bulb, to allow the shoots from the bulbs beneath to emerge between them.

6 Repeat this process, adding layers of compost and bulbs working from latest blooming at the bottom, to earlier blooming varieties at the top.

7 Finish by adding a layer of compost at least 5cm thick. Sprinkle horticultural grit on top if you have it, for extra protection.

8 Give your bulb lasagne a gentle water, then sit back and enjoy the magic! Your bulbs will emerge in succession, giving you months of colour and joy from late winter all the way through to summer.

1

2

3

4

5

CREATE NATURAL HERBAL FIRELIGHTERS

One of the greatest joys of the colder months is getting cosy around a fire. Whether you're lucky enough to have a log burner in your home, or gather friends around a fire in the garden, watching the flames flicker and feeling their warmth on a chilly evening is always so comforting. These natural firelighters make the ritual of lighting a fire even more special. I love making these at the time of year when the days are rapidly shortening and the weather feels a little gloomy. Making these helps me to slow down, notice the beauty in the small things and embrace the restful, cosy side of winter.

WHAT YOU'LL NEED
Saucepan and heat-safe bowl that sits on top
Wax pellets
Undyed cotton string, cut to 5cm pieces; or 5cm candle wicks
Egg carton and/or cardboard fruit tray
Tablespoon
Wood shavings or sawdust
Dried herbs e.g. rosemary, thyme, lavender
Dried flower petals e.g. rose petals, calendula petals, cornflowers
Spices e.g. cinnamon sticks, star anise, cloves

WHEN TO START
Any time

WHEN TO ENJOY
Year-round

1 Make a double boiler by adding water to a saucepan, then adding a heat-safe bowl that's large enough to sit on top without falling in. Fill the bowl with wax pellets, then place the pan on a low heat to bring the water to the boil. (Don't use your favourite bowl for this as the wax can be tricky to clean off.)

2 While your wax is melting, place a piece of string or a candle wick upright in the centre of a section of the egg carton or cardboard fruit tray. Next, add a tablespoon of wood shavings, a couple of sprigs of dried herbs, some dried flowers and some spices to hold the string in place.

3 Repeat with the rest of the sections of the egg carton or tray.

4 Once the wax is fully melted, carefully pour some wax into each section – you don't need to fill them to the top, just add enough to hold everything in place.

5 Once the wax has completely cooled and set, you can tear or cut your egg carton or tray into individual firelighters.

6 These are pretty enough to display until you're ready to use them to start cosy fires during the colder months.

MAKE WILDFLOWER SEED BOMBS

When most people think of sowing seeds and planting flowers, they usually think of spring. But autumn is the perfect time to sow wildflower seeds – the same time they would be falling to the ground in nature. I love the idea of sowing in autumn: when everything else in the garden is slowing down, it gives you another bit of beauty to look forward to the following year. These wildflower seed bombs are perfect for scattering in bare parts of the garden where you haven't got time to implement a rigid planting scheme. They provide a much-needed source of nectar and habitat for pollinators and other wildlife too.

WHAT YOU'LL NEED
Compost or soil
Plain flour
Wildflower seeds (or a foraged mix of seeds native to your area)
Water
Baking tray

WHEN TO START
Autumn

WHEN TO ENJOY
Enjoy scattering the seed bombs in autumn, and enjoy the blooms the following year

1 In a large mixing bowl, combine roughly ten parts compost or soil with one part flour.

2 Sprinkle in your wildflower seeds – ideally you want about ½ teaspoon of seeds per handful of the soil mixture.

3 Add water gradually, mixing as you go, until you get a sticky, dough-like consistency.

4 Pick up small handfuls of the mixture and shape into balls with your hands, about the size of a golf ball.

5 Lay them onto a baking tray and leave to dry at room temperature for a day.

6 Once dry, your seed bombs are ready to be thrown around the garden. Scatter them on bare patches of soil or grass, and let nature do the rest.

2

2

3

4

5

INFUSE YOUR OWN ROSEMARY HAIR OIL

Is there anything rosemary can't do? The herb has been used since ancient times for reducing muscle pain, improving memory and boosting mood. It's also said that rosemary can promote hair growth – a powerful property that this project harnesses. Making your own rosemary hair oil is a simple, satisfying project that brings the garden into your self-care routine. This two-ingredient recipe can improve the health of your scalp, enhance the shine of your hair and even stimulate hair growth.

WHAT YOU'LL NEED
A few sprigs of dried rosemary
A clean glass jar with lid
250ml extra virgin olive oil
A sieve
A small bottle or jar

WHEN TO START
Any time, although summer and autumn are ideal when rosemary is most abundant

WHEN TO ENJOY
Year-round

1 Gently crush the rosemary sprigs with your fingers, just enough to release their essential oils.

2 Place the rosemary in a clean, dry glass jar. Pour over the olive oil, making sure the herbs are completely submerged.

3 Close the jar and place on a sunny windowsill for a few weeks to infuse. Give it a shake every few days to help everything infuse nicely.

4 Once it's ready, strain through a sieve to remove the pieces of rosemary and discard. Pour your strained liquid into a clean bottle or jar to store.

5 Keep your rosemary oil in a cool, dark place and it should last for several months.

6 For hair growth, massage a few drops of rosemary oil into your scalp, leave overnight and rinse thoroughly in the morning.

7 To add shine, add a few drops to the ends of your hair.

1

2

3

CRAFT AN AUTUMN WREATH

You may associate wreaths with Christmas, but they have a long history of being used to mark the changing seasons. Making an autumn wreath is a beautiful way to celebrate the richness of this time of year and connect with nature. Foraging for little treasures to include in your wreath helps you to appreciate the small details of the natural world and to notice the tiny changes in the plants around you. The colours, textures and scents of autumn foliage and seedheads make this a lovely and calming sensory experience.

WHAT YOU'LL NEED
A selection of autumn leaves, seedheads, herbs, dried flowers, grasses etc (whatever you can forage from your garden or local area)
A wreath base (see Tip)
Secateurs or scissors
Twine
Ribbon or string

WHEN TO START
Early autumn

WHEN TO ENJOY
Throughout autumn into early winter

1 Collect your materials. Take a walk in your garden or local park and look in hedgerows to gather a variety of colourful leaves, seedheads and any other natural materials. Choose anything with a colour, shape or texture that appeals to you, making sure to forage sustainably and only take what's growing in abundance.

2 Start attaching the materials to your wreath base. Add the biggest items first, like the larger leaves, aiming to cover the whole base with these. Attach with twine.

3 Next, layer over the smaller materials, such as seedheads and dried flowers. Add as many of these as you like – these will help the wreath to look full and lush. Either poke them into the existing twine that's wrapped around the base or secure them with more twine.

4 Make any final adjustments until you're happy with your wreath. To hang, attach some ribbon or string. Display it on a door or wall, or wherever you'll walk past often.

TIP: You can make your own wreath base out of willow or hazel by twisting the stems into a circle. Using a natural material for the base means the whole thing is compostable and doesn't need to be taken apart after use.

CREATE A DIY HERB DRYER

In early autumn, there are still plenty of plants and herbs that can be harvested in the garden and foraged from your local area. As the days shorten and the weather cools, many plants will start to fade and the amount that can be harvested begins to shrink. Picking and preserving herbs now helps to make the most of what's growing before winter sets in. This DIY herb dryer is made from materials you might already have, or can easily get hold of second hand. It's the perfect low-effort way to dry your herbs, so you can enjoy their flavour through winter.

WHAT YOU'LL NEED
An old tea towel or scrap fabric
An embroidery hoop
Pen
Scissors
String

WHEN TO START
Any time, but best when you have an abundance of herbs to preserve

WHEN TO ENJOY
Year-round

1. Lay your tea towel down flat and place the embroidery hoop on top. Draw a circle around the embroidery hoop about 2cm wider than the hoop itself.

2. Cut the circle of fabric out of your tea towel.

3. Separate the outer and inner rings of the embroidery hoop.

4. Cut three 25cm pieces of string and tie to the outer hoop. Try and space these as evenly as possible. Tie the three pieces of string together at the top; this is to hang your herb dryer from.

5. Cut six 15cm pieces of string and tie these to the inner embroidery hoop; these are to hang bunches of herbs from.

6. Place the circle of fabric over the inner embroidery hoop, then put the outer embroidery hoop over the top. You may need to loosen this to get it over the additional fabric and string that's been added. Tighten the outer hoop to secure them together.

7. Hang your herb dryer in a well-ventilated spot out of direct sunlight.

8. Your herb dryer is now ready to use. You can add flower heads such as chamomile and calendula to the fabric layer to dry, and hang bunches of herbs and flowers like rosemary and lavender from the strings.

TIP: Attach multiple embroidery hoops together if you want space to dry more flower heads.

7

8

9

10

GROW A MUSHROOM TOWER

Mushrooms are the highlight of autumn for me. If there's one thing that gets me excited about this time of year, it's going on woodland walks on a drizzly day and seeing what mushrooms I can spot. However, most mushrooms aren't exactly beginner-friendly when it comes to foraging, so I mostly like to observe the ones I spot in the wild, leave them to drop their spores and reproduce, and grow my own at home. This project shows you one of the easiest ways to grow mushrooms outdoors, which is an extremely rewarding process.

WHAT YOU'LL NEED
15kg untreated straw
A large bucket or bin
3kg oyster mushroom spawn
A shady spot in your garden
2 large pieces of cardboard (about 1m^2)
5m length of chicken wire
String (optional)

WHEN TO START
Early autumn, when the weather is cool and damp

WHEN TO ENJOY
Autumn and early winter, or the following spring

1 Soak the straw in water overnight in a large bucket or bin.

2 Remove your mushroom spawn from the fridge to allow it to acclimatize for about an hour before using.

3 Find an area for your mushroom tower; it needs to be somewhere out of direct sunlight e.g. under a tree. Make sure the area is level and free from weeds.

4 Layer the pieces of cardboard on the ground and water them.

5 Wrap the length of chicken wire to form a double-layered tube, it should be about 80cm wide. Secure into place by either carefully bending the ends of wire, or tie into place with string. Stand the chicken wire tube on top of the cardboard.

6 Add a 20cm layer of soaked straw to the bottom of the tube.

7 With clean hands, break up about an eighth of the oyster mushroom spawn and sprinkle it on top of the straw.

8 Keep layering straw and mushroom spawn, pressing each layer of straw down as you go, until you reach the top of the tower, making sure you finish off with a thick layer of straw.

9 Compact everything down gently and give your tower a final gentle water to make sure everything is damp.

10 Keep watering your tower during dry spells to make sure it doesn't dry out, and you could get mushrooms in as little as six weeks.

START A TINY TREE NURSERY

As the Chinese proverb goes: 'The best time to plant a tree was 20 years ago, the second best time is now'. On autumn walks, you'll spot acorns, conkers or hazelnuts scattered beneath the trees. Gathering a few and starting your own tiny nursery may seem like a small act, but it could have a huge impact. Growing trees from seed is deeply grounding, you're nurturing something that will live for so many years to come, support wildlife, and could even provide shade for future generations. And these little saplings also make lovely living gifts for loved ones, that they can enjoy for many years too.

WHAT YOU'LL NEED
Acorns, conkers, hazelnuts or any other tree seeds you can find
A large bucket
Peat-free multipurpose compost
Garden soil or leaf mould
Small plant pots or containers (yogurt pots with holes cut in the bottom would work well)
Plant labels (see page 209 for DIY plant labels)
Permanent marker or pencil
A sheltered spot in your garden
Chicken wire or mesh

WHEN TO START
Autumn

WHEN TO ENJOY
For years to come!

1 Gather your seeds. I like to go on a long autumnal walk and collect fresh, plump undamaged seeds from under the trees.

2 In a bucket, mix together two parts multipurpose compost to one part garden soil or leaf mould.

3 Fill your pots with the compost mixture, leaving a little space at the top for easy watering.

4 Push the seeds into the pots of compost at a depth of about twice the size of the seed. Poke two into each pot, if both sprout, you can remove the weaker sapling later on.

5 Label each pot with the type of seed you've planted and the date and give them a gentle water.

6 The seeds need a period of cold weather to break their dormancy, so leave the pots outside over winter. Cover the pots with chicken wire or mesh to prevent squirrels digging up the seeds.

7 Water during dry spells and wait patiently for the shoots to emerge in spring.

WINTER

Winter is a season of rest and recovery, both for the garden and for us. As growth slows down, it's the perfect time to notice the little things — the beauty of frosted spiderwebs, buds full of potential on bare tree branches and the resilience of plants that survive through the harshest conditions. I try to get outdoors wherever I can, even for a short walk, to breathe in the fresh air and stay connected to nature. I love using this season to get creative with little projects that keep me feeling close to the garden until spring arrives.

CULTIVATE MUSHROOMS USING OLD COFFEE GROUNDS

This is a great project for anyone short on outdoor space. Growing mushrooms indoors can be done at any time of year, but it's particularly satisfying in winter when not much else is growing. The speed at which mushrooms grow makes cultivating them incredibly exciting; they literally double in size every day. Growing mushrooms on coffee grounds is also a great way to use a by-product that might otherwise go to waste. If you don't drink coffee, ask your local coffee shop: most give away their used grounds for free – just make sure they're from the last 24 hours (see box opposite).

WHAT YOU'LL NEED
Rubbing alcohol
Clean rubber gloves
Coffee grounds
A large bowl
100g grey, pearl, pink or white oyster mushroom grain spawn
Mushroom growbag (about 10 x 40 x 8.5cm)
Adhesive tape
Somewhere dark to keep the bag
Scissors
Spray bottle

WHEN TO START
Any time, but it makes an ideal winter project

WHEN TO ENJOY
Year-round

1 If your coffee grounds are frozen, remove from the freezer and allow to come to room temperature.

2 Sanitize your working area and equipment, and put on a pair of clean rubber gloves.

3 Add your coffee grounds to a large bowl, then crumble in the mushroom spawn, making sure to break it up into small pieces. Mix until the spawn is evenly distributed.

4 Add the coffee and spawn mixture to your mushroom growbag. Make sure the mixture doesn't go above the filter patch as air needs to circulate through here.

5 Leaving an air pocket of about 5cm in the top of the bag to allow the mycelium to breathe, fold the top of the bag closed and secure with tape.

6 Place the bag somewhere dark like a cupboard, ideally with a steady temperature of about 15–25°C. Keep an eye on the bag for the next few weeks.

7 After 2–3 weeks, the coffee grounds should have been completely colonized by mycelium – you'll know it has worked if the coffee grounds have turned white and started to solidify.

8 Remove the bag from its storage place, fold down the top of the bag to remove the air pocket and fix it down with tape. Cut an 'X' in the front, centre point of the bag with scissors, about 7cm wide. Place the bag somewhere light but out of direct sunlight.

9 Spray the 'X' opening with water at least twice a day to maintain humidity. You should start to see the pin heads of little baby mushrooms appear after a week or two. Continue to spray these twice a day until they are fully grown.

10 Harvest your homegrown mushrooms when the caps begin to flatten out by twisting off the whole cluster with your hand.

(3)

COLLECTING COFFEE GROUNDS

These need to be fresh to avoid contamination. If you're collecting your own, you can freeze them after brewing until you have collected 1kg. Coffee grounds from a French press/cafetière will contain too much water. If collecting grounds from a coffee shop, make sure they were brewed that day.

(4)

(8)

(9)

BUILD A BEE MANSION

Winter is the perfect time to build a bee mansion so it can be ready and waiting for when solitary bees emerge in spring. It's also a great time for collecting materials like fallen leaves and branches, which are perfect for making cosy little pockets of habitat. This design is made by stacking wooden pallets, which are easy to get for free, and filling the gaps with scavenged materials like bricks, sticks, bamboo and hollow stems, to create homes for all sorts of insects. If you don't have the space for a bee mansion of this size or access to pallets, you can scale it down to fit your space using the materials you can find. Whatever design you go for, you'll be helping to support the biodiversity of your garden for years to come, all from materials you already have lying around!

WHAT YOU'LL NEED
Sunny, sheltered area of garden
2–4 wooden pallets (roughly the same size so you can safely stack them)
Screws (optional)
A collection of natural materials of different shapes and sizes (see box)
Compost, old compost bag and pollinator-friendly plants (optional)

WHEN TO START
Winter or early spring

WHEN TO ENJOY
Year-round

1 Choose a sunny, sheltered area of your garden for your bee mansion.

2 Stack your pallets on level ground, making sure they're sturdy and won't fall over. If necessary, you could secure them together with screws.

3 Fill the gaps in the pallets by tucking natural materials between the layers to create different types of habitat for a variety of insects.

4 You could also line the gaps in the top pallet with old compost bags, and plant them up with pollinator-friendly plants.

5 Let nature move in, and see if you can spot anything buzzing or crawling around your bee mansion in spring.

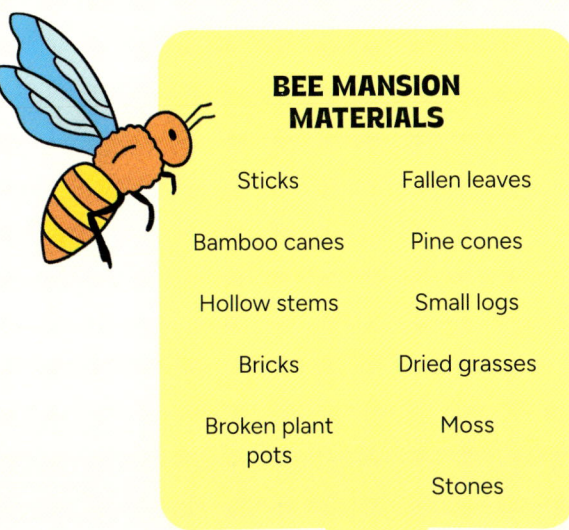

BEE MANSION MATERIALS

Sticks	Fallen leaves
Bamboo canes	Pine cones
Hollow stems	Small logs
Bricks	Dried grasses
Broken plant pots	Moss
	Stones

WINTER

CONSTRUCT A LIVING WILLOW DOME

Willow is such an amazing plant, and great for beginner gardeners. It just wants to grow and can thrive in a range of conditions. It's also flexible, fast-growing and easy to work with, which makes it perfect for weaving into domes, tunnels and archways. Planting willow in the winter while it's dormant gives it the best chance to root, ready to burst into life in spring. Planting a willow dome is a lovely way to create a calming hideaway in the garden as a peaceful reading spot or a natural den for kids to enjoy.

WHAT YOU'LL NEED
Sunny or partly shaded spot
Fresh willow rods, at least 1.8m long
Garden twine or string
Scissors
Mulch like bark or straw to retain moisture

WHEN TO START
Winter

WHEN TO ENJOY
Spring, when the willow comes to life, and through the rest of the seasons

1 Choose a spot for your living willow dome. Willow likes full sun or part shade, and thrives in damp areas.

2 Mark out a circle. A diameter of at least 1.5m will work well, but making it wider will give you more space inside to sit and relax. To get an even circle, push a stick into the ground as a centre point and tie string to it, cut to the length of your chosen radius. Walk the string around in a full circle, marking the ground as you go to outline where the rods will be planted.

3 Clear the area, removing weeds and grass so the willow doesn't have to compete with anything.

4 Plant the willow rods by pushing them into the ground at least 20cm deep at regular intervals, about 30–50cm apart. Angle them slightly towards the centre of the circle so it's easier to fix them together. Remember to leave a wider opening at the front for an entrance.

5 Bend the rods towards the centre of the circle, twist opposite rods around each other and secure in place with string. Make any adjustments until you're happy with the shape.

6 Give the willow a really deep water, and add a thick layer of mulch at the base of the stems to help retain moisture.

7 Watch the structure come to life in spring, and weave any new side shoots around each other to fill in the gaps in the dome, add more detail and strengthen the structure.

GROW MICROGREENS ON YOUR WINDOWSILL

Microgreens are the fastest way to get a homegrown harvest, perfect for impatient gardeners. They can be grown at any time of the year, but I love growing them in winter for instant gratification when it feels like everything else in the garden is moving slowly. The best thing about this project is you might already have everything you need in your house; you can upcycle old fruit punnets or milk cartons into the planters, and use ingredients from your kitchen cupboard like mustard seeds, lentils or chia seeds to grow microgreens from.

WHAT YOU'LL NEED
An old fruit punnet, milk carton or other shallow container with drainage holes
Scissors (optional)
Compost
Seeds (see opposite)
A spray bottle
A piece of cardboard that fits on top of the container
A plate to put your container on top of
A sunny windowsill

WHEN TO START
Any time

WHEN TO ENJOY
A week after sowing

1 Make sure the container you're using has drainage holes. If it doesn't, poke some in with a pair of scissors.

2 Fill the container almost all the way with compost and level it out.

3 Water the compost so it's damp but not soggy.

4 Scatter your seeds thickly on top of the compost – microgreens don't need much space to grow so you can cover almost the whole surface with seeds, just make sure they're not piled on top of each other.

5 Spray the seeds with water and cover with the piece of cardboard. You could add some weight on top of this, like a book or stack more containers of microgreens on top, as this mimics soil pressure and encourages strong germination.

6 Lift up the cover and check your seeds daily, give them a spray with water if the compost looks dry.

7 After a few days, you should see seeds starting to send out shoots and tiny leaves starting to form. Remove the cover and move them to a sunny windowsill. Continue to water lightly as they grow.

8 Harvest after they've developed their first set of true leaves (the second set of leaves that appear after the initial rounded seed leaves). Snip them just above the soil level and enjoy them sprinkled onto your meals as a garnish or as part of a salad.

SEEDS

From your kitchen cupboard:	From your seed box:
Mustard seeds	Kale
Chia seeds	Peas
Coriander seeds	Radishes
	Beetroot
Sunflower seeds	Basil
Lentils	Parsley

3

3

4

MAKE A WILDLIFE TEEPEE

We're not the only ones who appreciate a cosy shelter over winter – insects and garden wildlife are also looking for safe spaces to tuck themselves away during cold days and frosty nights. While it can be tempting to tidy everything up in the winter, sweeping leaves off flower beds or cutting down dead stems, one of the best things you can do for wildlife is leave behind cosy pockets of natural materials for them to hide in. That said, you might still end up with piles of prunings, leaves on paths and driveways, or simply prefer a tidy looking garden. This project is the perfect solution, as it helps to turn those materials into homes for wildlife, while keeping your space looking neat and tidy.

WHAT YOU'LL NEED
Three large sticks, as long as you want the height of your teepee to be
Garden twine or string
Scissors
A collection of natural materials from your garden e.g. leaves, sticks, straw, hollow stems, pine cones
Secateurs (optional)

WHEN TO START
Autumn or winter

WHEN TO ENJOY
Wildlife will start to move in straightaway

1 Push your long sticks about 20cm into the ground in a triangle shape. Tie the tops of the branches together with string or twine.

2 Place a layer of large sticks in the base of the teepee, trim them with secateurs if needed, so they fit inside the structure.

3 Pile up layers of leaves, sticks and other material inside the teepee to create as many little pockets for wildlife as possible. I like to place larger sticks around the edges to help hold some of the smaller material inside.

4 Once your teepee is full, leave it undisturbed for wildlife to move in. It won't take long for bugs to find it and call it their home.

5 You can either leave the teepee to compost down in situ over time, keep topping it up with material as it shrinks down, or gently move the contents to your compost heap once the weather has warmed up in spring.

CRAFT DIY BIRD FEEDERS

Watching birds in my garden is one of my simple pleasures. Birds need extra support during the colder months, when their natural food sources are scarce. By putting out feeders for them, not only are you helping them to survive the cold nights, but you also get to enjoy their cheerful presence in your garden. I like to place my bird feeders where I can view them out of a window, especially one that I would normally sit or stand in front of, like the window by my desk or kitchen sink. That way, I get to see them visit and enjoy the food I've put out for them, which makes me feel connected to nature even when I'm indoors.

WHAT YOU'LL NEED
An orange (you can also use lemons and limes to make mini feeders)
Spoon
A chopping board
A sharp knife
String or garden twine
Scissors
A stick to make a perch
Wild bird seed mix
Sheltered spot to hang your feeder

WHEN TO START
Winter – the earlier in the season, the better, to give the birds plenty of fuel to survive

WHEN TO ENJOY
Straightaway

1 Cut the orange in half on a chopping board. Scoop out the flesh and place into a bowl to eat later. You should be left with two empty cups of orange peel.

2 Using a knife, poke four holes at equal distances into each orange peel cup, about 1cm down from the rim.

3 Cut your string or twine into eight equal lengths, about 30cm long.

4 Poke the ends of the string through each hole in the orange peel and tie a knot at the end to secure in place. Tie the other ends of all four pieces of string together, trying to get them as even as possible. Push a short stick through the centre of the orange half to make a perch for the birds to sit on while they eat.

5 Fill your orange peel cups with wild bird seed mix.

6 Find a branch to hang your feeders from. Ideally in a sheltered spot where birds will feel safe to land, make sure they're hanging freely but aren't buffeted too much by the wind. Try to place the feeders out of reach of cats, and on a thin branch to help deter any squirrels.

7 Quietly observe the feeders – see if you can spot birds visiting and whether you can identify them.

8 Refill the feeders when they're empty. If you see signs of mould on the orange peel, compost it and make a new one.

1

1

3

4

MAKE A FORAGED CHRISTMAS WALL HANGING

I couldn't write a chapter of winter gardening projects without mentioning Christmas, could I? Even if this isn't something you celebrate, you can still mark the season by making your own foraged winter decorations. I love switching up the seasonal decor in my home and bringing the outside in helps me to feel more in tune with nature. I find this especially comforting in the winter, a time of year when I might not be spending as much time outdoors. This winter wall hanging is so simple to create and easily adjustable to what you can find near you.

WHAT YOU'LL NEED
Foraged natural materials of different shapes and textures
Secateurs
String or twine
A branch or piece of driftwood

WHEN TO START
Winter

WHEN TO ENJOY
Throughout winter

1 Forage for materials in your garden or local area. Look for a mixture of different shapes and textures. Remember to forage responsibly and only pick what's growing in abundance.

2 Cut your greenery to no longer than 10cm in length.

3 Gather small handfuls of greenery and any additional decorations (a few stems per bunch) and tie each bunch together with string, leaving plenty of excess string at one end.

4 Tie each bunch of greenery to the branch, spacing them evenly apart but at varying heights. You could also tie on individual decorations such as orange slices.

5 Fix your wall hanging either to the wall or ceiling to enjoy through the winter months and beyond.

TIP: To create a christmas wreath, use the instructions from Craft an Autumn Wreath (see page 159) and switch up the autumnal plants for seasonal festive ones.

SOW CHILLIES INDOORS FOR HOMEMADE HOT SAUCE

Towards the end of winter, I find myself itching to sow seeds again. Chilli plants are one of the first crops you can get started indoors; I usually sow mine in January and they're perfect for scratching that gardening itch while it's still too cold to get seeds started outside. Chillies really benefit from an early start, as they need a long season to grow in order to give us their fiery fruits in summer.

WHAT YOU'LL NEED
Seed tray or pots
Compost
Chilli seeds
A clear plastic bag or propagator lid
A warm sunny windowsill (above a radiator is ideal)

WHEN TO START
Late winter to early spring

WHEN TO ENJOY
Summer

1. Fill your seed tray or pots with compost, leaving 1cm space at the top, and firm down. Give the compost a gentle water so it's evenly moist but not soggy.

2. Put two seeds on the surface of the compost in each pot and cover them with a fine layer of compost, about 5mm deep.

3. Give the pots a very gentle water or spray and cover them with your plastic bag or propagator lid to maintain humidity.

4. Place in a warm spot, ideally 20–26°C, and make sure they don't dry out.

5. Check for seedlings. Once they appear (which can take anything from 1–6 weeks), move them to the brightest spot in your house.

6. Make sure the soil doesn't dry out, it's ideal to water them from below (place the pots in a shallow dish of water, which the plants will wick up via capillary action) to prevent the stems from rotting.

7. When the seedlings have their first sets of true leaves (the ones after the initial seed leaves), they can be moved into their own larger pots. If you planted two seeds into each pot and both germinated, remove the smaller, weaker seedling. Keep potting them on into bigger pots as they grow if you see signs of roots poking out the bottom of their pots.

8. Plant outside or into a greenhouse or polytunnel once all risk of frost has passed, or grow indoors on a sunny windowsill.

9. Harvest your chillies as soon as they ripen and use them to spice up your meals or make a delicious hot sauce (see page 198).

HOMEGROWN FERMENTED HOT SAUCE

One of the best things you can make with your homegrown chillies is this fermented hot sauce. The fermentation process gives this sauce such depth of flavour and the garlic makes it so addictive. Once you've tried this hot sauce, you'll want to drizzle it on every meal you make! The heat level of the sauce will totally depend on what chillies you use but, if you don't want it too spicy, you could always switch out some of the chillies for sweet peppers.

250g chillies (if you want a milder sauce, swap out half for bell peppers)
3 garlic cloves, peeled
1 tsp salt
60ml water
60ml raw apple cider vinegar

1 Add the chillies (and bell peppers if using), garlic, salt and water to a blender. Blitz until it looks like a chunky salsa.

2 Start the fermentation process by pouring the mixture into a clean glass jar. Cover with a tea towel. Leave out at room temperature for 1–2 days to begin fermentation.

3 Stir in the apple cider vinegar, re-cover and leave on the counter for a further 5–7 days.

4 After about a week, transfer the mixture to a blender and blitz until smooth.

5 Pour the mixture into a clean bottle or jar, it will keep in the fridge for several months.

WEAVE A RAISED BED

Taking a pile of sticks and transforming them into something beautiful and practical without having to spend a penny is pretty mind blowing for me. I absolutely love the way these raised beds, woven from natural materials, look. They add a soft, whimsical touch to any space. One of the best things about them is they can be built in any size and any rounded shape to fit your space. Winter and early spring are the perfect times to start this project, when you're pruning trees and have plenty of long flexible branches at hand.

WHAT YOU'LL NEED
Sturdy, straight poles cut to 60cm lengths (or longer if you want a tall bed)
A mallet
An axe (optional)
Long, flexible branches of hazel, willow, or dogwood (about 1–3cm diameter)
Secateurs
Organic matter
Compost

WHEN TO START
Winter to early spring, when deciduous trees have lost their leaves

WHEN TO ENJOY
For 7–10 years after building

1 Mark out the shape of your raised bed. Bear in mind that large beds will require lots of material to create, and sharp angles will be trickier to bend the branches around.

2 Push the thicker, sturdy poles into the ground at regular intervals around your shape. Make sure they're at least 20cm deep in the ground; you can use a mallet to help drive them in. If the ground is particularly solid, you may need to carve the ends of the poles into points using an axe.

3 Start weaving the longer sticks in and out of the uprights. Don't worry too much about the ends poking out, you can trim those off later.

4 Use your mallet to tap down each layer and keep everything nice and compacted.

5 Continue to layer up the sticks, making sure to stagger the ends, and alternate them so each upright has some branches on the inside and some on the outside.

6 Once you've reached your desired height, trim off any ends that are poking out to make everything look tidy.

7 Fill your bed. I like to use any organic matter I can find around the garden to fill the bottom half of the bed e.g. logs, grass cuttings, fallen leaves. I then top it with a layer of compost.

8 You can plant into your beds straightaway, and enjoy them for years to come.

PROPAGATE YOUR HOUSEPLANTS

Long before I discovered the joy of gardening outdoors, I fell in love with houseplants. For anyone with little or no outside space, they're the perfect way to start growing. Houseplants teach you how to observe plants, the signs to look for when a plant is stressed or needs water, and they still let you get your hands in the soil, which is beneficial to your mental health. Houseplants also help to bring your space to life, boosting your mood and reducing stress levels. If you've already got one or two house plants, this project teaches you how to multiply them for free. You can use them to fill your space with more greenery or pass them on as gifts for friends or loved ones. If you don't already have house plants, don't worry, most plant lovers are happy to share a cutting or two.

WHAT YOU'LL NEED
Scissors or secateurs
A healthy houseplant to take cuttings from
A clean glass, jar or bottle
9cm plant pots
Peat-free multipurpose compost

WHEN TO START
Any time

WHEN TO ENJOY
Once the cutting has rooted, about four weeks

1 Using your scissors or secateurs, cut your houseplant at a 45 degree angle just below a node (this is the point where leaves attach to the stem). Aim for a cutting at least 10cm long with several healthy leaves.

2 Remove the lower leaves so none of them will sit in water, as these will rot. Make sure you still have 2–3 healthy leaves at the top.

3 Fill half a glass, jar or bottle with water and place your cutting in.

4 Put the glass, jar or bottle somewhere warm and bright but out of direct sunlight.

5 Every few days, empty the glass and replace the water.

6 After a couple of weeks, you should start to see white fresh roots beginning to grow from the node. Be patient as some plants will take a lot longer to root than others.

7 Once the roots have grown to 2–5cm long, you can plant it into a pot of compost.

8 Water the compost, keeping it moist but not soggy, and keep the plant somewhere warm and bright.

1

2

4

CRAFT WOODEN PLANT LABELS

I don't class myself as a very handy person – I'm not great at building or fixing things, but there is definitely a certain kind of satisfaction that comes from creating something with your hands. That's why I love this project so much: you get to make something truly useful (and free) with your hands, but it's so simple and doesn't require any fancy tools. These plant labels have a rustic charm to them, are a nice alternative to plastic labels, and can be made from leftover tree prunings or sticks that you find lying around. This project is evergreen and can be done at any time of year.

WHAT YOU'LL NEED
Sticks of at least 1cm diameter
A sharp knife – a pen knife/Swiss Army knife/whittling knife would work
Secateurs or loppers strong enough to cut through your sticks
Permanent marker, pencil or pyrography (wood-burning) tool

WHEN TO START
Any time

WHEN TO ENJOY
Straightaway

1 Gather your sticks (I like to use prunings from my hazel tree but just look for any fresh sticks that have at least a 1cm diameter) and cut them to your desired length. I make mine about 20cm long.

2 Hold one end of your stick, with the other end facing away from you.

3 Dig your knife into the stick about 5cm from the far end and shave away a layer of bark, making sure to push the knife away from you. Continue to shave off strips of wood until you have a flat surface that's wide enough to write on.

4 Repeat with more sticks, to make as many labels as you'd like.

5 Write your plant names on the labels with either a fine permanent marker, pencil or burn them on with a pyrography tool – this option is longer lasting but requires additional equipment and is more time-consuming.

INDEX

A
acorns, natural dyes 100–3
aloe vera, health effects 51
aluminium salts 100
annuals 22
archways 'Secret Garden' 48–9
autumn wreath 159–61
avocado, natural dyes 100–3

B
bacteria, soil 10
balconies 12
bath soaks 86–7
bee mansion 176–7
beetroot, chioggia 60
bird feeders, DIY 190–1
borage
herbal teas 94–5
sowing 71
brain, gardening benefits 10
Brussels sprouts 122
budgeting 7
bulbs
bulb lasagne 144
planting 140–1

C
calendula
bath soaks 86
health effects 51
herbal teas 94–5
lip balm 82
salad bar, grow your own 104–5
sowing 70
carrots
Christmas dinner 121
purple 62
chamomile
bath soaks 86
growing from a tea bag 28–9
health effects 51
herbal pathway 116–17
herbal teas 94–5
natural dyes 100–3
chillies
homegrown fermented hot sauce 198
sowing and growing 196
chioggia beetroot 60

chives 70
Christmas dinner, grow your own 120–3
Christmas wall hanging, foraged 192–3
climbing plants
'Secret Garden' archway 48–9
sweet pea teepee 66–7
clothes, natural dyes 100–3
cocktail garden 34–5
cocktails, lemon verbena mojito 38–9
coffee grounds mushroom cultivation 174–5
compost 21
worm composting bin 136–7
container pond 96–9
control, letting go of 18
cornflowers 71
cosmetics, lip balm 82
costs 7
courgettes, pizza or pasta garden 126–9
cucumbers, white 63

D
dome, living willow 178–9
dopamine 10
drainage 21
drinks
herbal teas 94–5
homegrown fizzy 88–9
lemon verbena mojito 38–9
dyes from plants 100–3

E
echinacea, herbal teas 94–5
edible flowers 70–1
elderberries, natural dyes 100–3
exercise 10–11

F
fennel
herbal teas 94–5
use by witches 56
fermented foods and drinks
homegrown fermented hot sauce 198

homegrown fizzy drinks 88–9
firelighters, herbal 148–9
flowers
bulbs 140–1, 144–5
DIY flower press 132–3
edible 70–1
fabric flower hammering 112–15
night scented garden 131
sweet pea teepee 66–7
wildflower seed bombs 152–3
foxgloves 56
frost dates 22

G
ginger, homegrown fizzy drinks 88–9
glossary 21–2
gratitude 14
green and mood 10
gut microbiome 88

H
hair oil, rosemary 154–5
Halloween pumpkins 54–5
hardening off 22
healing windowsill garden 50–1
herbs
bath soaks 86–7
cocktail garden 34–5
DIY dryer 162–3
healing windowsill garden 50–1
herbal firelighters 148–9
herbal pathway 116–17
lip balm 82
smudge sticks 74–5
tea garden 94–5
hope 11
hormones 10
houseplants, propagating 206–7

I
insect bath, olla 108–9
irrigation, ollas 108

K
kalettes 122

212 INDEX

L

labels, wooden plant 208–9
lavender
  bath soaks 86
  herbal pathway 116–17
  herbal teas 94–5
  sleep pouches 92–3
  smudge sticks 74–5
layering 12
lemon balm
  bath soaks 86
  health effects 51
  herbal pathway 116–17
  herbal teas 94–5
lemon verbena
  herbal teas 94–5
  lemon verbena mojito 38–9
lettuce 105
lip balm 82
living willow dome 178–9

M

mashua 62
material
  dyes from plants 100–3
  fabric flower hammering 112–15
meadowsweet 86
memory
  gardening benefits 10
  nostalgia patch 46–7
microgreens, growing on windowsill 182–3
mindfulness
  gardening 10
  smudge sticks 74–5
mint
  bath soaks 86
  health effects 51
  herbal pathway 116–17
  herbal teas 94–5
  planting 35
mistakes, learning from 18
mojito, lemon verbena 38–9
mood-boosting tea 95
mordant 100
moths 131
mugwort
  smudge sticks 74–5

use by witches 56
mulch 21–2
mullein 86
mushrooms
  coffee grounds cultivation 174–5
  mushroom tower 164–5
  mycelium plant pots 68–9
  mycelium plant pots 68–9
  Mycobacterium vaccae 10

N

nasturtiums
  natural dyes 100–3
  salad bar, grow your own 104–5
  sowing 71
nature, connecting with 10, 14
nettles 100–3
night scented garden 131
nostalgia patch 46–7

O

oca 60
olla insect bath 108–9
onion skins, natural dyes 100–3

P

paper, wildflower seed 42–5
parsnips 121
pasta garden 126–9
pathway, herbal 116–17
peppers, pizza or pasta garden 126–9
perennials 22
pizza garden 126–9
plant labels, wooden 208–9
pollinators
  general attraction tips 14–15
  night scented garden 131
  planting a patch 32–3
pond, container 96–9
poppy 56
potatoes 122
pots, grow your own from mycelium 68–9
pots, grow your own, olla insect bath 108–9
pressed flowers 132–3
probiotics 88

propagating houseplants 206–7
pumpkin growing 54–5

R

radishes 105
raised beds, weaving 202–3
recipes
  herbal teas 94–5
  homegrown fermented hot sauce 198
  homegrown fizzy drinks 88–9
  lemon verbena mojito 38–9
  relaxing tea 95
resilience 18
rose 86
rosemary
  hair oil 154–5
  smudge sticks 74–5

S

sage
  herbal pathway 116–17
  herbal teas 94–5
  smudge sticks 74–5
  use by witches 56
salads
  grow your own salad bar 104–5
  growing microgreens 182–3
The Secret Garden (film) 48
seeds
  sowing 22
  tree nursery 168
  wildflower seed bombs 152–3
  wildflower seed paper 42–5
self-confidence 7, 10
serotonin 10
shade gardens 76–7
sleep pouches, lavender 92–3
smudge sticks 74–5
soil
  bacteria 10
  free draining 21
soothing digestive tea 95
sowing seeds 22
space 12
sunflower growing challenge 40–1
sweet pea teepee 66–7

T

tea bags, growing chamomile from 28–9
teepees
sweet pea 66–7
wildlife 186–8
thinning out 22
thyme
health effects 51
herbal pathway 116–17
smudge sticks 74–5
toiletries
bath soaks 86–7
lip balm 82
rosemary hair oil 154–5
tomatoes
pizza or pasta garden 126–9
rainbow 63
tree nursery 168

V

vegetables
Christmas dinner, grow your own 120–3
growing microgreens 182–3
pizza or pasta garden 126–9
salad bar, grow your own 104–5
weird and wonderful 60–3
violas 70

W

watering 22
wildflower seed bombs 152–3
wildflower seed paper 42–5
wildlife
bee mansion 176–7
container pond 97
DIY bird feeders 190–1
general attraction tips 14–15
night scented garden 131
olla insect bath 108
wildlife teepee 186–8
willow dome, living 178–9
windowsills
growing microgreens 182–3
healing garden 50–1
witch's gardens 56
wooden plant labels 208–9

worm composting bin 136–7
wreathes
autumn 159–61
Christmas 193

Y

yarrow 56

INDEX 215

ACKNOWLEDGEMENTS

This book began as just a small seed of an idea and thanks to so many kind and talented people it has grown into something real. The purpose of this book has always been to share the mental health benefits of gardening, and I couldn't have done that without so many supportive people around me, both personally and professionally.

First and foremost, I'd like to thank the lovely Emily Barrett, my literary agent, for being with me from day one, helping me believe in this idea and showing me how to navigate the new-to-me world of publishing. Without her, I probably would've gotten overwhelmed and given up!

Speaking of publishing, I'd of course love to thank Ellen Simmons and Alice Kennedy-Owen from Pavillion, who have been so passionate about the book from the beginning, and have helped bring it to life. It's been a pleasure to work on this with you.

It's been such a joy to work with India Hobson, who took all of the beautiful photos in this book! I'm blown away by her talent and so pleased with how everything came together.

I'm endlessly thankful to all of my friends and family for putting up with my slow replies while I was working on this, and for continuing to cheer me on every step of the way.

I also want to thank Poppy and Seth who kindly let me grow on their land while I wrote this book – thanks for letting me create all these gardening projects around your space!

To my followers and community at @inthecottagegarden – thank you so much for your enthusiasm and support. You remind me every day why I love sharing the joy of gardening.

And, finally, to all the plants, gardens and wild spaces have taught me so much – thank you for keeping me grounded.

ABOUT THE AUTHOR

Amy Chapman started gardening when she bought her little cottage in the countryside of West Wales, complete with stream and ducks. She has a particular interest in organic, regenerative vegetable growing and creative gardening projects. Having grown up in a working-class family, Amy is devoted to sharing accessible projects which can be done in a small space and on a budget. Amy is passionate about reaching people who aren't currently gardeners, offering them a unique perspective and new ideas to get them hooked on gardening, so that they too can reap the benefits that it brings.

Pavilion
An imprint of HarperCollins*Publishers* Ltd
1 London Bridge Street
London SE1 9GF

www.harpercollins.co.uk

HarperCollinsPublishers
Macken House
39/40 Mayor Street Upper
Dublin 1
D01 C9W8
Ireland

10 9 8 7 6 5 4 3 2 1

First published in Great Britain by Pavilion
An imprint of HarperCollins*Publishers* 2026

Copyright © Pavilion 2026
Text © Amy Chapman 2026

Amy Chapman asserts the moral right to be identified as the author of this work. A catalogue record of this book is available from the British Library.

ISBN 978-0-00-8603755

Publishing Director: Laura Russell
Commissioning Editor: Ellen Simmons
Design Manager: Alice Kennedy-Owen
Editorial Assistant: Daisy Gudmunsen
Production Controller: Grace O'Byrne
Layout Designer: maru studio G.K.
Illustrator: Rosie Barker
Photographer: India Hobson
Copyeditor: Molly Price
Proof-reader: Vicky Orchard
Indexer: Ruth Ellis
Reproduction: Rival Colour Ltd, UK

Printed and bound by GPS Internationale Handels Holding GmbH

All rights reserved. No part of this publication may be reproduced, stored in a retrieval system, or transmitted, in any form or by any means, electronic, mechanical, photocopying, recording or otherwise, without the prior written permission of the publishers.

Without limiting the exclusive rights of any author, contributor or the publisher of this publication, any unauthorized use of this publication to train generative artificial intelligence (AI) technologies is expressly prohibited. HarperCollins also exercise their rights under Article 4(3) of the Digital Single Market Directive 2019/790 and expressly reserve this publication from the text and data mining exception.

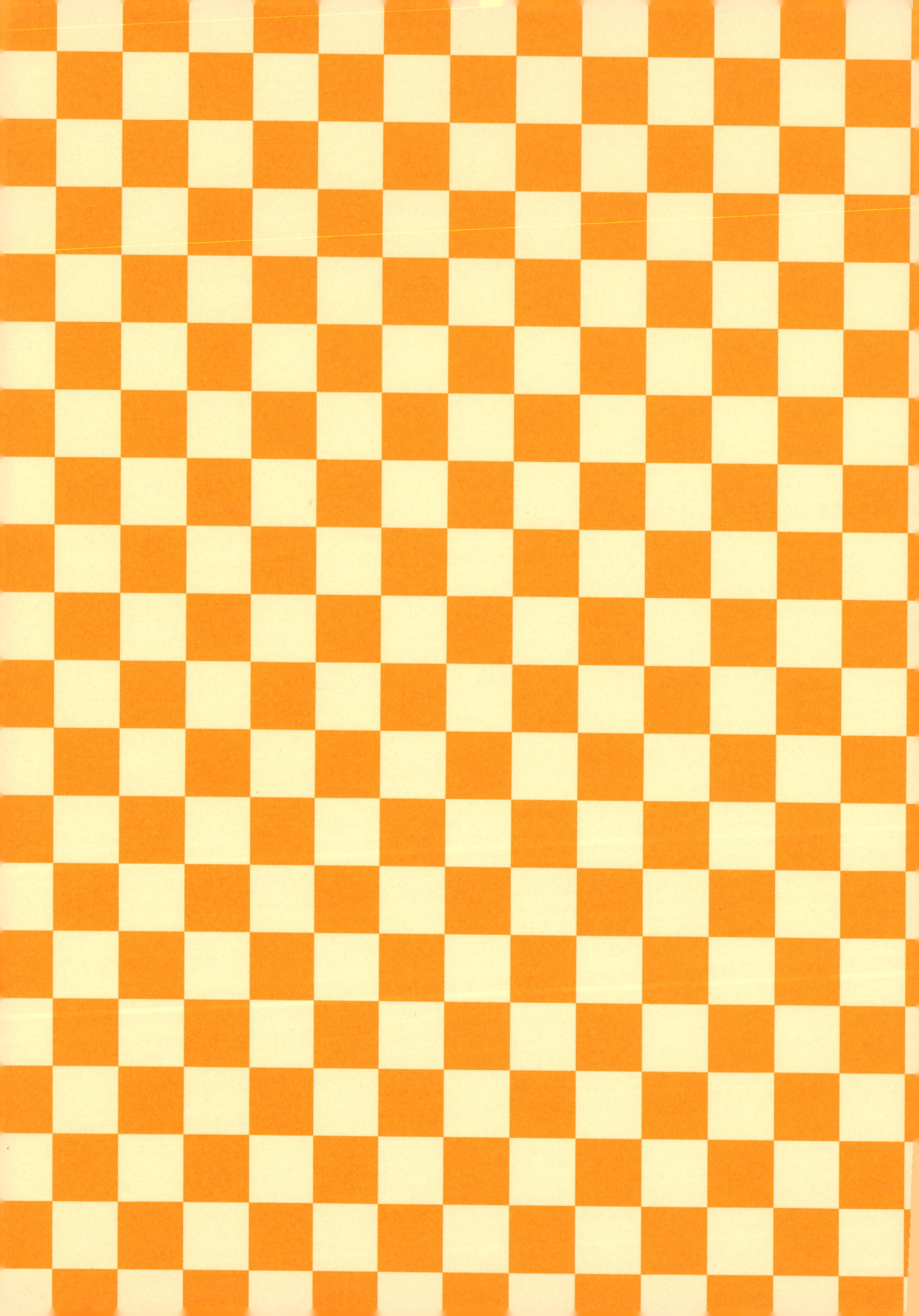